THE

LOCOMOTIVE ENGINE:

INCLUDING

A DESCRIPTION OF ITS STRUCTURE,

RULES FOR ESTIMATING ITS CAPABILITIES,

AND

PRACTICAL OBSERVATIONS ON ITS CONSTRUCTION AND MANAGEMENT.

BY ZERAH COLBURN.

BOSTON:
REDDING AND COMPANY, NO. 8 STATE STREET.
1851.

INTRODUCTORY NOTICE.

The absence of any purely practical work on American Locomotives has induced the preparation of the following pages devoted to that subject. It is believed the book will afford to the student a clear idea of the nature and mode of application of steam power, while to those engaged in the manufacture and operation of engines it will afford much useful matter connected with their construction and management.

Much care has been bestowed to render plain and distinct those parts of the book which are devoted to the principles of locomotive science, and the rules and illustrations have been adapted to the wants of those who have but little time or taste for the pursuit of abstract investigations. While this feature will constitute a chief merit of the work in the hands of such persons, it will make it none the less definite and exact for the purposes of the designer and engineer.

The particulars of many recent engines, and improvements connected therewith, have been presented, embracing the patterns of a majority of all the builders in the United States. For many of these we are indebted to the manufacturers of engines, while others have been procured for the purpose from the engines themselves; those machines being selected which presented some new or favorable features in the proportions of their parts or in the arrangement of their machinery.

It is therefore hoped that the book may impart some benefit to those who read it, and that it may serve to this purpose until the appearance of a better one from those whose opportunities for information would enable them to treat the subject in a manner more suited to the various requirements of its nature.

THE

LOCOMOTIVE ENGINE.

SECTION I.

The Properties of Steam and the Phenomena connected with its Generation.

THE most prominent of the properties possessed by steam are, its high, expansive force, its property of condensation by an abstraction of its temperature, its concealed or undeveloped heat, and the inverted ratio of its pressure to the space which it occupies.

Steam is the result of a combination of water with a certain amount of heat; and the expansive force of steam arises from the absence of cohesion between and among the particles of water. Heat universally expands all matter within its influence, whether solid or fluid; but in a solid body it has the cohesion of the particles to overcome, and this so circumscribes its effects that in cast iron, for instance, a rate of temperature above the freezing point sufficient to melt it, causes an extension of only about one-eighth of an inch in a foot. With water, however, a temperature of 212°, or 180° above the freezing point, (and which is far from a red heat,) converts it into steam of 1700 times its original bulk or volume.

All bodies may exist in either one or all of three different states, viz.: the solid state, the liquid state, and the aeriform state, or state of vapor. Water, for example, may exist as ice, liquid, and steam; and the condition which it assumes depends on its pervading temperature.

Steam cannot mix with air while its pressure exceeds that of the atmosphere, and it is this property, with that which makes the condition of a body dependent on its temperature, that explains the condensing property of steam. In a cylinder once filled with steam of a pressure of 15 lbs. or more to the square inch, all air is excluded. Now as the existence of the steam depends on its temperature, by abstracting that temperature (which may be done by immersing the cylinder in cold water or in cold air,) the contained steam assumes the state due to the reduced temperature, and this state will be water. And, as the water cannot occupy the volume which it did under its former temperature, it follows that its reduction in volume must remain a vacuum. A cylinder, therefore, filled with hot steam, may be condensed by an abstraction of its heat, and a vacuum will be produced in the cylinder with a few drops of water at the bottom, which may be pumped out by an air-tight pump, leaving the vacuum perfect.

When this principle is employed in removing the atmospheric pressure opposed to the back of the piston in a steam engine, such an engine is termed a condensing engine; and in such engines more work may be done with the same pressure of steam, than by a non-condensing engine, as the absence of the weight of the air, or the negative pressure on the back of the piston is equivalent to a positive pressure on the other side, and contributes by so much to the useful effect of the engine. Locomotive engines, however, and most American stationary engines, discharge their steam without condensing, and to overcome the atmospheric resistance they carry higher steam ; they are therefore called high pressure engines.

The next property of steam which we have mentioned, is that of its latent or concealed heat. An unknown amount of latent heat exists in every element in nature : thus iron becomes hot by merely hammering it on an anvil ; air gives off heat enough to light fire by being compressed into a syringe, and so on. The beating of the iron does not *create* the heat which it excites, neither does the compressing of the air ; they both merely *develop* the heat, which must have a previous existence. In these examples the heat which is excited is freed by the *motion* communicated, — and we have no means of knowing its amount ; — but the latent heat of steam, though showing no effects on the thermometer, may be as easily known as the sensible or perceivable heat. To show this property of steam by experiment, place an indefinite amount of water in a closed vessel, and let a pipe, proceeding from its upper part, communicate with another vessel, which should be open, and, for convenience of illustration, shall contain just 5½ lbs. of water at 32°, or just freezing. The pipe from the closed vessel must reach nearly to the bottom of the open one. By boiling the water contained in the first vessel until steam enough has passed through the pipe to raise the water in the open vessel to the boiling point, (212°,) we shall find the weight of the water contained by the latter to be 6½ lbs. Now this addition of one pound to its weight has resulted solely from the admission of steam to it ; and this pound of steam, therefore, retaining its own temperature of 212°, has raised 5½ lbs. of water, 180°, or an equivalent to 990° ; and including its own temperature we have 1202°, which it must have possessed at first.

The sum of the latent and sensible heat of steam is

in all cases nearly constant, and does not vary much from 1200°. It is from this property of steam that it becomes of such essential service in heating buildings; one square foot of superficial surface of cast iron steam pipe will keep 200 cubic feet of air at a congenial summer heat; but a square foot of the surface of a bar of iron, of the same *perceivable* temperature, would scarcely start the frost on the windows in a cold morning.

If a known volume of steam of a certain pressure be made to occupy but one-half that volume, its elastic force will be doubled; or, in other words, the same pressure is exerted within one-half the original capacity. By pressure we mean the initial elastic force of the steam, which is always the same in equal weights of steam, and which can only act with greater intensity of pressure by restricting the area exposed to its action. In fact, it is an established law of steam, and of all elastic fluids generally, that the pressure which they exert is inversely as the space occupied; or, to be more precise, it is very nearly so. At the end of the present section we shall give a table of the temperature and elastic force of steam, which will show the exact increase of pressure corresponding with any diminution in bulk.

The elasticity of steam increases with an increase in the temperature applied, but not in the same ratio. If steam is generating from water at a temperature which gives it the same pressure as the atmosphere, an additional temperature of 38° will give it the pressure of two atmospheres; a still further addition of 42° gives it the tension of *four* atmospheres, and with each successive addition of temperature, of between 40° and 50°, the pressure becomes *doubled*. It is well for the student of the steam engine to know the reason of this effect, and we will endeavor to explain it. We have already said that there is no *cohesion* among the particles of fluids, but there is, however, an *attraction* between all matter in nature. The action of heat in generating steam has to overcome this attraction among the particles of the water; and likewise the *gravity* of the water itself. As the water becomes rarified by heat, and either in its natural state, or as steam, occupies a greater volume, this attraction is diminished, and also the weight or gravity of the water; hence an additional rate of temperature does not have to contend with the same resistance as the temperature which preceded it, and is, therefore, enabled to produce greater effects in the generation of steam.

Among a variety of facts and notes relative to the nature of steam, we select the following: —

If water be boiled in an open vessel, no temperature greater than that for the boiling point (which for *fresh* water is 212°,) can be produced in it. All the surplus heat which may be applied passes off in the steam.

If the vessel be closed, and the steam as it is formed be retained within it, the temperature may be raised, and retained in the steam.

If the steam, as it is formed, is allowed to accumulate in the boiler, its pressure on the water level makes an increased temperature necessary to continue its production.

Steam, in itself, is invisible, and becomes visible only upon condensation, as when a jet is discharged into the open air; — its loss of temperature causes it to condense, and we see it in the form of a vapory cloud.

In treating with steam, the term *heat* is understood as expressing its sensible heat, while the term *caloric* provides for the expression of every conceivable existence of temperature.

To explain the theory of ebullition, or boiling liquids, we will observe that in metals, heat is communicated by the conducting property they possess; but in liquids it is communicated by a circulation of particles. If heat be applied to the bottom and sides of a vessel containing water, that portion of the water in contact with the heated metal becomes heated and rarified, and consequently lighter than the rest, whereby it ascends to the surface, gives off its vapor, becomes cooled, and in consequence becoming heavier, descends, again to become heated, rise, and descend as before, and to maintain these operations in a constant succession so long as the heat is applied. This action is performed in vertical planes, and if the heat be applied above the bottom of the vessel, the water below that point will receive but little heat, and can never be made to boil.

An established relation must exist between the temperature and elasticity of steam; in other words, water at 212° must be under the pressure of the steam naturally resulting from that temperature, and so at any other temperature.

If this natural pressure on the surface of the water be removed without a corresponding reduction in the temperature, a violent ebullition at the water-level is the immediate result. Thus, suppose the entire steam room in a boiler to be six cubic feet, and the contents of the cylinder which it supplies to be two cubic feet; at each stroke of the piston one-third of all the steam in the boiler is discharged, and the surface of the water is consequently relieved from one-third of the pressure upon it before that stroke. The temperature remains the same, but as it does not bear the natural relation to this diminished pressure, it causes the water to boil violently, and produces *foaming*. Foaming is a cause of which priming (or working water along with the steam into the cylinders,) is the effect. Provision must therefore be made in all boilers, that they may have a large extent of steam room compared with the cylinders which they supply.

Another result attending the formation of steam is, that when an engine is in operation and working off a proper supply of steam, the water-level in the boiler artificially rises, and shows by the gauge-cocks a supply greater than that which really exists. This is owing to the steam forming in the water and rising in bubbles to the surface, and displacing by its bulk the amount of water indicated by the *rise* at the gauge-cocks. As the production of steam under the same temperature cannot continue under an increased pressure, it follows that when the discharge of steam is stopped, and its entire pressure is thrown on the surface of the water, steam is no longer generated, and the water takes its natural level.

At whatever point in a boiler steam be taken, there is a determination of water to that point, which is occasioned by the sudden reduction in the pressure, owing to the withdrawal of the steam. This is the case with all boilers having steam domes with throttles in the same; and it was for this reason that on a new engine lately constructed at the Eastern Rail Road Shop, at East Boston, the steam dome was omitted, and in its stead a steam pipe, perforated on its upper side, was extended the whole length of the boiler, occupying the position usually given to the steam-pipe in ordinary locomotives. The object of this was to take the steam alike from all parts of the steam room of the boiler, so that no rise of water should result at any one point.

Notes.—One cubic foot of atmospheric air weighs 527.04 Troy grains, while an equal bulk of steam at 212° weighs 258.3 grains; the specific gravity, therefore, of steam at the pressure of the atmosphere, and taking that of the atmosphere at 1, is .490.

The force of steam is the same at the boiling point of every fluid.

27.104 cubic feet of steam at the pressure of the atmosphere, equal 1 lb. avoirdupois.

TABLE OF THE TEMPERATURE AND ELASTIC FORCE OF STEAM; ALSO THE VOLUME OF STEAM GENERATED, COMPARED WITH THE QUANTITY OF WATER FROM WHICH IT IS RAISED AT DIFFERENT PRESSURES.

[*Note.*—Steam, raised from water at 212°, has no pressure above that of the atmosphere, and can produce no useful effect except in obtaining a vacuum in a condensing engine. If admitted to one end of a cylinder it would expel the air, and would there remain without producing any motion, unless the pressure of the atmosphere on the back of the piston was removed. In this table we have therefore given the temperature corresponding with the steam at pressures *above* that of the atmosphere. We would also here remark that the pressure in a locomotive or other boiler, as indicated by the safety valve, is the real pressure *above* the atmosphere, as the air presses upon the top of the valve with the same force as a corresponding pressure of steam within. In a boiler showing 50 lbs. pressure per square inch, by the safety valve, there is a pressure of 65 lbs. — 15 lbs. of which are expended in overcoming the pressure of the air on the top of the valve. Therefore, the remaining 50 lbs., indicated by the valve, is the effective pressure for a non-condensing engine, although a condensing engine would realize nearly the full effect of 65 lbs.]

Pressure in lbs. above the atmosphere, and also including the same.		Temperature in deg. Fahrenheit.	Volume of steam compared with that of the water from which it is raised.
30 lbs.	45 lbs.	276.4	610
40 "	55 "	289.3	508
50 "	65 "	301.3	437
60 "	75 "	311.2	383
70 "	85 "	320.1	342
80 "	95 "	328.2	310
90 "	105 "	335.5	282
100 "	115 "	342.5	260
110 "	125 "	349.0	241
120 "	135 "	355.1	225
130 "	145 "	360.7	211
140 "	155 "	366.2	198

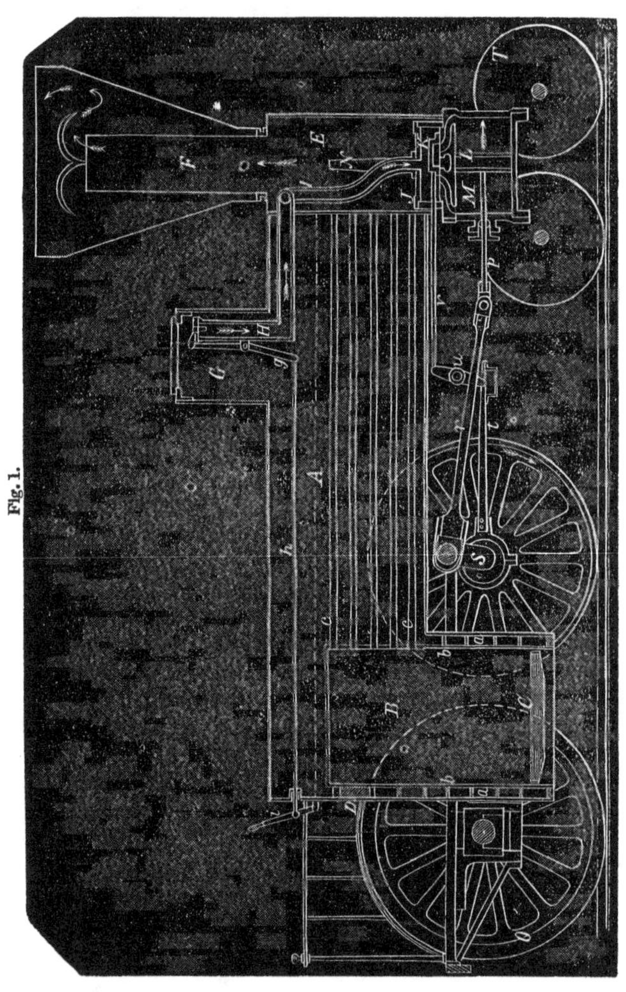

Fig. 1.

SECTION II.

A General Description of the Construction of the Locomotive Engine.

HAVING illustrated the prominent properties of steam, it remains to show in what manner its useful effect may be realized in the production of power for locomotive purposes. Any reader would be aware that a locomotive must combine within itself the means for the generation of steam, its application to produce motion within the machine itself, and also the propulsion of the whole upon the road. A complete locomotive steam engine, therefore, combines three distinct arrangements for realizing these conditions. The source of power lies in the boiler and fire-box; the cylinders, valves, piston, and the connections, are the means by which it is applied to produce motion within the machine; and the wheels, by their tractive force or adhesion to the rails, secure the locomotion of the machinery which impels them, and also, from their surplus power above what is necessary to move the engine alone, the draught of a great load upon the rails. It is therefore necessary to understand the construction of each of these parts, and also the general arrangement by which they are combined in the production of power.

A reference to the figure on the opposite page will serve to show the construction of an ordinary eight-wheeled engine, as divided in the direction of the length of the boiler so as to show the entire machinery for generating and applying the power.

The boiler, A, in which the steam is first produced,

is of a cylindrical form, having a furnace or fire-box, B, at one end, surrounded by a water casing, *a, a,* communicating with the boiler, and which is to prevent the destruction of the plates of which the fire-box is formed by the intense heat of the fire. The plates which form the outside of this water casing are united to the cylindrical part of the boiler, and form what is called the outside fire-box. This outside fire-box supports the furnace or fire-box proper by a number of stay bolts, seen at *b, b;* these bolts being screwed at their ends into the sides of both fire-boxes. C is the grate, the bottom of the fire-box being open to admit the air necessary for the combustion of the fuel, and D is the door through which the fuel is admitted. At *c, c,* are shown a number of small copper tubes, their purpose being to convey the heated air through the boiler, from the fire-box to the smoke-box, E. The arrangement of these tubes may be better understood by an inspection of Fig. 2, which shows the fire-box and boiler divided transversely across its diameter. They are very small, and are placed so as to be but $\frac{5}{8}$ of an inch apart in any direction. They are also very thin, so as to communicate the heat passing through them to the water which surrounds them, and which generally stands four or five inches above their upper or top row. It is the surface of the fire-box and the exterior surfaces of these tubes that constitute the heating surface of the boiler. That portion of the boiler above the water-level, (which is shown by the dotted line,) is the steam room of the boiler, and is occupied by the steam generated from the water above and among the tubes and in the water space around the fire-box. The forward compartment of the boiler, or smoke-box, at E, receives the surplus of heated air not communicated to the water, and the gaseous products of the combustion of the fuel in the fire-box; and the chimney, F, provides for their escape

Fig. 2.

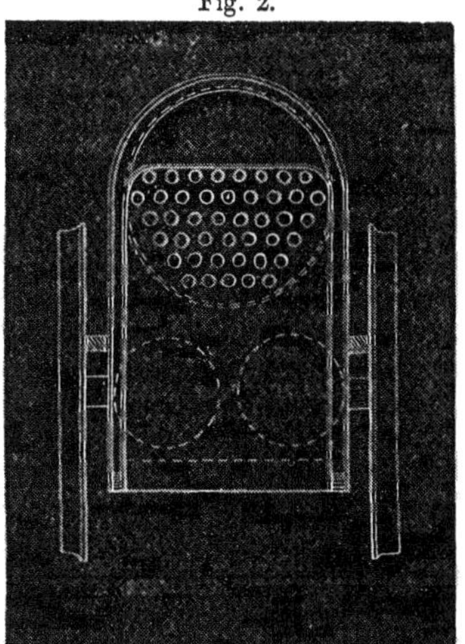

into the open air. The draught of the fire through the tubes is excited artificially by the escape of the steam from the cylinders of the engine, the arrangement and operation of which we shall explain hereafter. This, then, is the arrangement by which the power applied to produce locomotion is first generated. The peculiar form given to the boiler, the contact of water with the sides and top of the fire-box, and the great extent of heating surface afforded by the disposition of the tubes, secure the rapid production of a vast volume of steam within very restricted limits. In future pages we shall explain numerous details and appendages belonging to the boiler, and shall give its best proportions, as, likewise, of every other part connected with the engine.

The second division of the entire arrangement of the engine is that in which the power already generated is applied to produce motion within the machine. Upon the top of the boiler a cylindrical chamber or dome, G, is formed, and the pipe which conveys the steam from the boiler, penetrates it as seen at H. The object of elevating the mouth of the steam feed-pipe is to prevent the motion of the engine from throwing particles of water into it, to be carried into the cylinders and to oppose a load to the motion of the engine. The mouth of this pipe is covered by a valve, provided with ports or openings to admit steam within it, and the admission of steam is governed by the motion communicated to the valve, through its lever, *g*, rod, *h*, and starting lever, *i*, without the boiler and accessible from the footboard, where the engineer or driver stands. In the figure this valve is represented open, and the steam is descending through the pipe, in which it passes along through the partition between the boiler and smoke-box and down through the branch-pipe, I, into the steam chest, J. This steam chest communicates with each end of the cylinder, M, by the passages seen in the figure, and steam is admitted through these passages* alternately to each end of the cylinder by a sliding valve, seen at K. Within the cylinder is a piston, L, against which the pressure of the steam is exerted to produce motion. In the position given to the valve, K, in the figure, the left hand passage is open and is admitting steam to that end of the cylinder, to press the piston in the direction of the arrow. There is also a quantity of steam on the right hand of the piston, which was employed in the preceding stroke to force the piston to the left hand of the cylinder; and its work being now done, it is escaping through the right hand passage, and turning in a cavity in the under side of the valve into a third passage on the face of the cylinder, and which is situated between the two induction passages, already mentioned. The exhaust steam is carried in this last pas-

* Described as induction ports.

sage a short distance around the cylinder, and passes through an opening on the side of the same, into the bottom of a vertical pipe, part of which is seen at N. The mouth of this pipe is considerably contracted, as seen in the figure, and the resistance given by this contraction to the exit of the steam, makes it discharge in a very forcible blast. This powerful draught at the mouth of the tubes excites the passage of the heated air through them, and causes a great intensity in the fire. Without this artificial draught the boiler could not, from its proportions of fire surface, generate sufficient steam to supply the cylinders.

We have seen the steam entering by the left hand passage within the cylinder, and impelling the piston towards the opposite end of the same. As the piston approaches the right hand termination of its stroke, the valve K is made to shift its position in the steam chest, and to close the left hand passage, and likewise, by the same motion, to open the opposite or right hand one. The left hand passage is fully closed when the piston is within three or four inches of the end of the cylinder, and the right hand passage almost at the same instant begins to open, so that the full pressure of steam is exerted against the right hand side of the piston before it actually has completed its stroke in that direction. This advance of the valve on the piston is termed the *lead* of the valve, and when confined within certain limits is found to increase the speed of the engine, as it allows the steam to act with a concussive force, like that of a spring, at the ends of the strokes, so as to lose no time in changing the motion of the piston. When the piston has commenced on its return stroke, and while it is in its motion, the valve moves likewise in the same direction, uncovering the right hand passage more and more, until, when the piston has returned to the position shown in the figure, or to the middle of the stroke, this passage is fully open; the same as the left hand passage shown in the figure to admit steam for the preceding stroke. The motion of the valve has transferred the cavity on its under side to the left hand passage, and the steam, which during the preceding stroke was admitted through that passage, will now discharge through it, and pass into the exhaust port and up the exhaust pipe, N, as already described. By the time the piston has reached the middle of its stroke, the valve will have reached the end of its motion on the face of the cylinder, and will begin to move the contrary way, so that during the last half of the stroke of the piston, the piston and valve move in opposite directions.

The cavity on the under side of the valve, in which the steam turns from the induction into the eduction port, must receive such a width of opening as to allow the exhaust steam to *commence* its escape from one end of the cylinder before steam is admitted to the opposite end; so that if, for instance, the lead of the valve on the induction side be ⅛ of an inch, the exhaust must have a lead of about ¼ inch. In other words, when one steam port is taking steam through ⅛ of an inch, the other port must be discharging steam through ¼ of an inch. This is necessary for the free escape of the steam, that it may oppose no load to the progress of the engine.

We are now to show how the motion of the piston is communicated to the wheels, and in what manner the sliding valve, K, is moved within the steam chest, so as to regulate the admission of steam to the cylinder; and to guard against any misconception on the part of the reader, we will say here that there are two steam chests and two valves and cylinders, together with two entire but similar arrangements for communicating the power exerted against the pistons to the wheels. The figure does not admit of the representation of but one *engine*, (the cylinder and its valve and piston being the engine,) the other being behind the one we have shown. The steam pipe, H, after passing through the partition between the boiler and smoke-box, is divided into two smaller pipes, one of which conveys the steam to each cylinder.

Within the centre of the body of the piston is keyed the rod, P, which passes through a stuffing-box in the cover of the cylinder, and is attached at its other end to a cross-head having a pin or bearing for a connecting rod. This cross-head is also attached to guides to ensure the motion of the piston-rod in the line of the axis of the cylinder. The connecting rod, *r*, takes hold of this pin at one end, and at the other to a wrist or bearing of the crank axle, *s*, upon the extremities of which axle, are keyed the driving wheels of the engine. As there are two cylinders and connecting rods, there are necessarily two cranks in this axle, and they are placed at right angles, one with the other, so that one piston may be exerting its entire force against it, while the other is changing the direction of its motion, and is exerting but comparatively little power.

The alternate motion of the pistons is thus converted into a continuous circular motion, and it is from this motion that the movement for operating the valves is derived in the following manner. Four eccentric pulleys, the action of which is the same as that of short cranks, are affixed to the axle between the two cranks. There are two eccentrics for each cylinder; one being set at such an angle with the crank for that cylinder as to give the proper motion to the valve for a forward motion of the engine, and the other to produce a backward or retrograde motion. These eccentrics are encircled each with a brass strap, to which is attached a rod, *t*, having a hook at its remote end. At *u*, is a rocker shaft provided with arms on its upper and lower sides. If the hook of the forward eccentric rod be dropped on a pin in the lower arm, the motion of the forward eccentric will be communicated to the valve through the rocker shaft, *u*, and its upper arm, and the valve stem, *v*. And so of the hook in the backward eccentric rod. Another shaft mounted with arms or cambs, and governed by a lever within reach of the engineer, is made to throw out either the forward or backward or all the hooks in the eccentric rods. This shaft is laid immediately beneath the hooks, and traverses in the same direction as the rocker shaft, *u*.

It will now be easy to trace the operation of the steam, and of the machinery put in motion by its action on the piston. The throttle valve at the mouth of the steam pipe, H, being open by the lever, *i*, the steam will be admitted to within the pipe, and will descend through it and through the branch pipe, I, into the steam chest, J. From here it will find its way into the cylinder through whichever passage that may be open, and as that is here the left hand one, it will be admitted to press against the left hand side of the piston, and to move it towards the opposite end of the cylinder, by which time the right hand passage will have been open to admit steam to force the piston back again. The motion of the piston will be communicated to the axle of the driving wheels, through the piston rod, *p*, connecting rod, *r*, and crank, *s*; and the motion so transmitted will cause the eccentrics to turn, and by their motion to operate the valve through the eccentric rod, *t*, rocker shaft and arms, *u*, and valve stem, *v*, so as to maintain the admission of steam to the cylinder in the manner described. The driving wheels, as they are turned, will by their adhesion to the rails move along the engine and its load; and the constant recurrence of these motions in the piston, valve, and their subordinate connections, will maintain the action necessary to produce this required progressive motion of the machine.

Of the remaining parts of the engine, O shows an additional pair of driving wheels, connected with those fixed to the crank axle, and turning with them. The object of this second pair of wheels is to obtain a greater adhesion to the rails than with only one pair, and also to relieve the principal pair of drivers from the great weight of the engine, which would otherwise come upon them—at least, all that portion not supported by the truck wheels, T. The drivers on the crank axle generally have plain rims, while those on the hind axle have flanges on their inner sides, as likewise the forward or truck wheels, in order to keep the engine on the the rails. The four forward wheels are combined in a separate frame which turns around a pintal secured to the body of the engine, and is to facilitate the passage of the engine around curves. There are springs over the bearings of the wheels to relieve the engine from shocks arising from inequalities passed over on the rails. There are pumps which are not shown in the figure, for supplying the boiler with water, as it is evaporated in the production of steam. These are of the forcing kind and are attached to the cross-head or to a pin on the outside of the driving wheels.

The boiler is provided with a pair of safety valves to provide for the escape of steam when it attains an unnecessary pressure, and the engine has also a whistle and bell for alarms and signals. Many recent engines have expansion or cut-off valves, the use of which we shall hereafter explain.

From what we have said we believe any one may acquaint himself with the general arrangement and operation of the locomotive engine. Our remarks on future pages will explain various details which would embarrass the reader on a first introduction to the machine, but which will serve to extend his acquaintance after he has mastered the leading principles of its action. The principal features of the engine, including the construction of the boiler and the operation of the steam in the cylinders, are universally the same, but there are various modifications in the arrangement of the subsidiary machinery, which distinguish the engines of different builders, without affecting, however, the purposes for which they are employed.

SECTION III.

Details of the Locomotive Engine. The Boiler and its Appendages.

There are several essential requisites which locomotive boilers must possess, among which are strength, lightness, and efficient qualities for the production of steam; and these requisites can only be obtained by giving very particular attention to the material of which a boiler is made, and of the manner in which it is manufactured.

Owing to the diminished strength of large boilers compared with small ones, the diameter is very rarely made greater than 4 feet outside of the iron. The plates of which the cylindrical part of the boiler and the fire-box are formed, are from $\frac{5}{16}$ inch to $\frac{3}{8}$ inch thick. Lowmoor iron is generally preferred; and the quality of the iron is determined by its general appearance and its established reputation among builders and others. We have, however, much American iron of a very excellent quality, which comes to the boiler maker entirely warranted by responsible dealers. Angle iron is often used to connect the cylindrical part of the boiler to the outside fire-box, and to the smoke-box. The selection of this iron requires some skill and experience, as much of it is liable to be *reedy* in its structure; and for this reason some builders obtain the proper flanges for joining the boiler to the fire and smoke boxes by turning over the edge of the boiler plate of which the shell is formed. The rivets about locomotive boilers are from $\frac{5}{8}$ inch to $\frac{3}{4}$ inch in diameter, and have a pitch of $1\frac{3}{4}$ inches, more or less. The stay bolts to secure the inside fire-box are for the most part $\frac{3}{4}$ inch in diameter, and $4\frac{1}{2}$ inches apart. These stay bolts are tapped into the inside and outside fire-boxes and are then riveted at each end. Their diameter and number should depend somewhat on the width of the water space around the fire-box; for if this be pretty wide, they must necessarily be long in proportion to their diameter. The usual number of stay rods in a boiler is 6 or 7 for a 40-inch boiler, and a greater number as the diameter of the boiler is increased. These rods are $\frac{7}{8}$ inch to an inch in diameter, and are tapped through the back sheet or sheet next to the foot-board of the fire-box, and through the back sheet also of the smoke-box, and then have a large nut screwed tightly up at the smoke-box end, (there being a head at the fire-box end,) and having a little red lead putty interposed between the nut and the boiler plate to insure a tight joint. Some makers employ right and left nuts in these rods, to draw them up to a proper strain, but these are hardly necessary. The bars to stay the crown of the fire-box are generally 5 or 6 in number, and are 2 inches thick, and from $2\frac{1}{2}$ to 3 inches deep. These bars must rest upon the top of the fire-box only at their ends, a space of $\frac{1}{4}$ to $\frac{3}{8}$ inch being left all along their under edges, to prevent the crown sheet of the fire-box from becoming burnt through, owing to an absence of water at those points. At the points, however, where they are riveted to the crown sheet, washers or thimbles must be placed in this space for the rivets to pass through, in order that they may have a bearing and not spring up the crown sheet.

In all ordinary boilers where wood is used as fuel, all parts of the boiler, with the exception of the tube plate at the fire-box end, are formed of iron. These tube plates, by many makers, are made of copper.

Hinkley's tube plates are $\frac{3}{4}$ inch thick. In Winans' Coal Engines, however, the fire-box is made of $\frac{2}{3}$ inch copper, and the tube sheet of $\frac{1}{2}$ inch iron. The tubes are also of wrought iron.

The tubes in wood engines are made mostly of No. 14 copper, their outside diameter being usually $1\frac{3}{4}$ in. Wrought iron thimbles for tubes are used by most builders, generally at the fire-box end, but in some cases at both ends of the tubes. We could point to some engines having no thimbles at either end of the tubes, and which show as tight joints as many engines having thimbles. Much, indeed, depends upon the management of a boiler. If an engineman is in the habit of putting out his fire by throwing two or three buckets of water into the fire-box on every slight emergency, or running with the door open to regulate the fire, the contraction produced in such cases by the sudden cooling of the flue sheets often works nearly every tube loose.

A method of tightening tubes has been used by the Lowell Machine Shop, which has given good results. It is to take a short piece, say 2 inches in length, of No. 14 copper tube, and of such diameter as to allow of its just sliding into the mouth of the boiler tube; it is firmly united to the latter by a brazed joint an inch long. What remains of the short tube projecting out is passed through the tube sheet, which is drilled to receive it, and the portion projecting beyond the tube sheet, is then turned over and headed in the usual manner. This brings the end of the boiler tube up to a tight bearing with the inside of the tube sheet.

With long copper tubes it is sometimes deemed advisable to give them a middle bearing, for which purpose a sheet is placed midway of their length and passing up high enough to support the top row. Our opinion, however, is, that these intermediate flue sheets intercept the circulation of the water, and in some cases occasion priming. We have observed this to be the case in some of Norris's engines, which, having tubes 10 ft. 8 in. long, were provided with these extra supports.

The braces which support the boiler and serve to connect it to the frame, are made either round or flat. When made round, they are made about 2¼ inches in diameter, and are turned, which adds much to their appearance.

The angle iron which secures the fire-box to the frame should extend the whole length of the fire-box, if there is nothing in the way to prevent it. It should be screwed tightly to the frame, and the screws to fasten it to the fire-box should pass through the water space, being tapped through both sheets. The heads of these screws should project outward considerably, as they are difficult to unscrew when it becomes necessary to remove them. There should be two rows of screws passing into the fire-box, one above the other; and the distance between the screws should be just sufficient to enable a wrench to be readily introduced to turn them.

The grates are always of cast iron, and are generally 4 inches deep at the center. Their thickness is about ⅝ of an inch on their upper edge, and ⅜ inch at the bottom. The space between them is ¾ inch. We know of one or two engines which were found to make steam much better by placing a piece of plate iron, six or eight inches wide, across the fire-box at that end of the grates next the tube sheet. By admitting air through the whole extent of grate surface, a large quantity of cold air naturally passes up close to the side of the fire-box, below the tubes, the draft being strongest there, and, from not passing directly through the fire, escapes into the tubes before it is properly heated. As this cools the tubes, it consequently checks the formation of steam; therefore, by not admitting the air beneath the ends of the tubes, but causing all the air to pass directly through the fire, it was found that more steam could be produced with the same fuel.

The grate should be a very few inches above the bottom of the water space around the fire-box, in order that the water below it may remain quiescent and collect any sediment that may deposit itself there.

The junction of the inner and outer fire-box at the bottom of the water space, is made with a bar of wrought iron 1½ inches thick, having rivets passed through it and headed on the outside of the fire-box sheets. Some, however, bend the sheet of the inner fire-box outward, until it meets that of the outer fire-box, and then rivet them together. This method, though cheaper, does not allow the water spaces to be so readily cleared of mud and deposit.

Norris and some other southern builders construct their boilers with the top of the fire-box worked into a hemispherical form, and having a small cast iron dome placed upon the top. This makes a very high dome, and gives a large amount of steam room, but this form of fire-box has several disadvantages, among which is the extra expense of a boiler constructed in this way, there being work about the fire-box which can be done only by very skilful workmen, and requiring much more riveting. Again; the height of the dome is liable to make the engine top-heavy, which, in engines having large wheels, and having the boiler set pretty well up, is quite a serious objection. The dome, also, from exposing so large an extent of heated surface, makes the interior of the "cab," over the footboard, insufferably hot, which is by no means a trifling matter to a man who has to stand in its heat for several hours together. With all this the size of the dome obstructs the look-out of the engineman, and the diagonal brace necessary to steady it, lies directly in his way. With all these objections against it, this form of dome can hardly be said to possess any advantages over the old-fashioned wagon-top fire-box, having a low cylindrical dome; although it is generally considered that drier steam can be worked from a "dome boiler," as these boilers are termed.

Hinkley forms a cylindrical dome, about 22 inches in diameter and 18 inches in height, about midway on the boiler between the fire-box and smoke-box. This dome has a cast iron cover of sufficient thickness to withstand the pressure of the steam, and of such size that the aperture which it closes may admit a man to the interior of the boiler. The steam pipe and throttle are placed on one side of the dome, so as not to obstruct the passage. The dome is made of the same iron as the shell of the boiler, is lagged, and covered with sheet iron in the same manner, and has a thin cast iron base and cap.

It is believed by many that a point near the smoke-box end of the boiler is the most favorable place from which to take the steam, as it is considered that the water is not in so violent a state of ebullition at that point as at the fire-box end.

Locomotives generally have two safety valves; one of 2¼ inches in diameter, next the footboard, and one of 3½ in. diameter, at the forward end of the boiler. We see no reason for this difference of size, unless the safety valve next the footboard cannot have a lever long enough for a larger valve without it projects out in the way of the engineman. The lever could be turned to one side, and thus admit the use of a larger valve. Large valves of 3½ inches or 4 inches in diameter are less liable to stick, as their bearing surfaces increase only directly as their diameters, while the pressures upon them increase directly as their *squares*. Thus a four-inch valve has but *twice* the bearing surface or circumference of a two-inch valve, while the pressure on it would be *four times* greater. A mitre bevel, which is the bevel usually given to the safety valves, seems too sharp. Were the bevel an angle of about 30°, that is to say having $\frac{1}{4}$ inch depth to $\frac{1}{2}$ inch width of valve seat, there would be no difficulty with the valves as to *sticking*.

The whistles used on many locomotives are of very heavy tone, and are 6 inches in diameter. These whistles have a valve stem passing down through the centre and operated by a bent lever outside. The exit passage of the steam from the lower cup, should be about $\frac{1}{32}$ inch in width, while the bottom of the upper cup should be chamfered on the inside so as to bring it nearly to a sharp edge. This sharp edge of the upper cup should be placed directly over the annular opening in the lower cup, that the steam from the latter may impinge directly upon it. A whistle $4\frac{1}{2}$ inches in diameter, and of the composition of which clock bells are made, gives a very clear and sonorous sound. The upper cup, however, is most commonly made of sheet brass or copper.

The spark arresters in general use on New England locomotives are the common bonnet sparker, the Patent sparker of French and Baird of Philadelphia, and Cutting's sparker. The bonnet sparker is the most common. A chimney of sheet iron, about 4 feet in height, is placed over the opening in the smoke-box, and a curved cast iron disc is placed immediately over this chimney. The cinders and sparks projected by the blast pipes against this disc, receive from the form given to it a change in their motion, which throws them down between the bottom of the chimney and the outer casing surrounding it. The smoke and steam also receive this motion, but readily rise, and, passing around the disc, come out through a wire netting at the top, This wire netting is to throw down such sparks as might have been carried with the steam, and would otherwise have been thrown out upon the track, becoming a source of danger to bridges and buildings along the line. A pipe sometimes leads from the bottom of the outer casing of the sparker to a spark-box on the front or sides of the smoke-box. This box, we believe, is termed the "Sub Treasury."

French and Baird's sparker, and Cutting's sparker, are not in so general use as the bonnet sparker, and could not be readily understood without the aid of engravings showing their structure.

The opening made for the chimney in the top of the smoke-box is about the same size as the diameter of the cylinder of the engine. The following rule, however, will be found to apply in all wood engines: Divide the number of square inches in the grate by 7.5, and the quotient expresses the area of the chimney in square inches.

Example. What should be the diameter of a chimney for a boiler having a grate 34 inches by 35 inches?

34
35

7.5)1190(158.6, Area of chimney.

And by calculation we find the nearest corresponding diameter to this area to be 14¼ inches.

The ash pan of a boiler is a plate iron tray, suspended by hooks or latches to the bottom of the fire-box, and should have a clear depth of 9 inches—the front side being left open to admit the air to the grates. The mouth or open side of the ash pan should be provided with a wire netting, and a damper of plate iron turning on a hinge should be fixed to draw up at pleasure by a small chain passing up to the footboard.

The gauge-cocks are three in number, and are on the hind sheet of the fire-box, within reach of the engineman. They must communicate with the boiler at such a point, that should the water chance to fall a trifle below the lower cock, the upper row of tubes shall not be uncovered. In ascending a grade of 80 feet per mile, the water at the fire-box end would stand two inches higher above the tubes than at the smoke-box end; the gauge-cocks should therefore communicate with the boiler at so high a point that neither end of the tubes could become uncovered under any ordinary circumstances without their giving warning of it.

The English have always used glass gauge-tubes in addition to the three gauge-cocks, but one tried on an engine on the Maine road broke in the first trial. To stand the action of the steam, the interior of the tube should be round, not formed like a thermometer tube, and the bore of the tube should not exceed $\frac{3}{16}$ inch; the glass should be thick and well annealed, and there should be an expansion joint at the upper end of it. If these conditions are observed, glass gauge-tubes can be used here as well as in England.

The blow-off cocks of locomotives should be on the back side of the fire-box, to prevent the steam and water escaping by them from blowing up sand into the bearings of the engine.

The mud-hole plugs are of brass, and are about $1\frac{3}{4}$ inches in diameter, and are tapped into the outer fire-box at the bottom of the water space. They should have stout square heads, as it is very difficult to turn them out when they have been a short time in use.

Having thus explained the details and uses of the boiler and its appendages, we will proceed to give the proportions adopted by different makers.

The table of dimensions given on the next page includes two of Hinkley's patterns, two of the Lowell Machine Shop engines, and also of Souther's 15 in. cylinder pattern.

PRINCIPAL DIMENSIONS OF FIVE DIFFERENT PATTERNS OF LOCOMOTIVE ENGINES.

Builders.	Boston Loc. Wks. for 6 feet gauge.	Hinkley & Drury.	Lowell Machine Shop.	Lowell Machine Shop.	John Souther.
Diameter of Cylinder,	15 in.	$13\frac{1}{2}$ in.	$15\frac{1}{2}$ in.	14 in.	15 in.
Stroke of Piston,	20 "	20 "	18 "	18 "	20 "
Diam. of Drivers,	5 feet.	$4\frac{1}{2}$ feet.	$5\frac{1}{2}$ feet.	5 feet.	$5\frac{1}{2}$ feet.
Diam. inside of Boiler,	44 in.	37 in.	43 in.	40 in.	42 in.
Length of Tubes,	11 feet.	$9\frac{1}{2}$ feet.	11 feet.	10 feet.	$10\frac{1}{2}$ feet.
Number of do.	141	88	140	119	135
Outside diam. of do.	$1\frac{3}{4}$ in.	2 in.	2 in.	2 in.	$1\frac{3}{4}$ in.
Length of Grate,	36 "	30 "	$31\frac{1}{2}$ "	34 "	37 "
Width do.	40 "	39 "	$36\frac{1}{2}$ "	35 "	$37\frac{1}{2}$ "
Depth of Fire-box,	$50\frac{1}{2}$ "	36 "	53 "	$48\frac{1}{2}$ "	53 "
Tube Surface, sq. feet,	710.9	437.5	806.3	623	649.42
Fire-box, " "	56.74	39.33	56.4	52.67	60.8
Area of Grate, "	9.74	8.12	8	8.25	9.63
Water Room, cub. feet,	69.6	40.6	69.0	56.6	
Steam do "	41	32.1	41.5	33.2	
Size of Steam Ports,	$10\frac{1}{16}$ x $1\frac{5}{16}$ in.		10 x 1 in.	10 x $1\frac{1}{4}$ in.	$9\frac{7}{8}$ x 1
" Exhaust do.	$10\frac{1}{16}$ x $1\frac{11}{16}$ "		10 x $2\frac{1}{8}$ "	10 x $2\frac{1}{4}$ "	$9\frac{7}{8}$ x $1\frac{1}{2}$
Position of Cylinders,	inside.	outside.	inside.	inside.	inside.

The 15-inch cylinder machines built at Taunton have 726 sq. ft. of tube surface, 11.23 sq. ft. of grate, and steam ports 14 by 1 in. The performance of these engines (with blast pipes 2⅜ in. at the mouth) is very superior. The Taunton Company give the largest proportion of heating surface to a given capacity of cylinder of any of the engine builders in New England.

In giving the fire-box surface, we have reckoned every inch of surface above the grate, deducting only for the tubes and the door. It is of course plain that all this surface is in contact with the water in the boiler, although it is customary among engineers not to include any portion of that side of the fire-box next the tubes as heating surface.

It will be seen from the table that Hinkley's 15-inch cylinder engine has the greatest extent of heating surface, compared with its capacity of cylinder, of the five engines given; and as the proportions adopted appear to answer very well, we will give the multipliers which will give the same proportions for any other size of cylinder.

Multiply the square of the diameter of the cylinder by 3.159, to get the heating surface of the tubes:
by .252, to get the heating surface in the fire-box:
by .0433, to get the area of grate:
by .309, to get the cubic feet of water room in the boiler:
by .182, to get the cubic feet of steam room in the boiler.

All the engines of which proportions are given in the preceding table, have four driving wheels and truck, with the exception of the engine by Hinkley & Drury, having 13½ inch cylinders; — this engine has four driving wheels, upon which the whole weight of the engine rests.

An engine lately constructed by Robert Stephenson & Co., Newcastle upon Tyne, England, may be taken in comparison with the foregoing.

This engine had two pair of 5-feet drivers, and one pair of leading wheels:

14-inch cylinder:

21-inch stroke:

50 square feet fire surface in fire-box:

9.91 " " " " on grate:

640 " " " " in tubes:

76.86 cubic feet water in boiler and around fire-box:

43 " " steam in boiler and dome:

7.5 " " steam used at one rev. of drivers.

As a further illustration of English locomotives, we will give the dimensions of an engine built by Bury, Curtis and Kennedy, of Liverpool, for the Birmingham and Shrewsbury (narrow gauge) Railway.

15-inch cylinder; 20-inch stroke; one pair of 5 ft. 7 in. driving wheels; one pair 4 ft. 1 in. leading, and one pair 3 ft. 7 in. trailing wheels.

Boiler shell 47 inches, smallest inside diameter, and containing 172 $1\frac{3}{4}$-inch tubes, 11 ft. 6 in.l ong. Grate, $50\frac{1}{2}$ in. long, by 42 in. wide, and 55 inches from crown sheet.

Induction ports, 12 by $1\frac{5}{16}$ in. Exhaust port, $3\frac{1}{4}$ in. wide. Single blast pipe, $4\frac{1}{2}$ in. at mouth. Cylinders, $23\frac{1}{2}$ in. between centers. Bearings of driving axle, 8 in. long, and 7 in. in diameter.

The heating surface of locomotive boilers has of late years been considerably increased, not only having been extended with the enlargement of the cylinders, but in a much higher ratio. In some recent 17-inch cylinder engines, constructed at Taunton, for the New York and Erie Railroad, the fire-box surface included about 90 square feet, while the tube surface fell but little short of 1000 superficial feet.

We will add a few particulars of an engine for burning bituminous coal, which was constructed for the Baltimore and Ohio Railroad, by Thacher Perkins, master of machinery on that road. The performance of this engine during the year 1849 was upwards of 23,000 miles, and was higher than that of any other first class engine on that road for the same time.

The diameter of the cylinder was 17 inches; stroke of piston 22 inches; four pairs of driving wheels having chilled *tires* 43 inches in diameter. The diameter of the boiler was 44 inches, and there were 125 wrought iron tubes, 12 feet 6 inches long, and $2\frac{1}{8}$ diameter at the fire-box end, and $2\frac{3}{8}$ diameter at the smoke-box ends of same. The grate was $37\frac{1}{2}$ inches long, by $41\frac{1}{2}$ inches wide, and the inside depth from crown sheet to grate was 50 inches. Attached to the boiler of this engine was the patent apparatus for heating the feed water by the surplus exhaust steam of the engine, which was invented by Mr. Perkins. The exhaust steam from both cylinders enters a square box in the center of the smoke-box. In this box is a movable valve by which the steam can be discharged through the ordinary blast pipes, or turned into a pipe leading to a steam casing surrounding the smoke-box. This pipe also continues along beneath the boiler, and is united to a steam belt surrounding the same at the fire-box end, and from which the steam finally escapes through a pipe for that purpose. The feed water can be admitted directly to the boiler, near the fire-box end of this pipe, or, which is intended in running, it can be pumped into a casing surrounding this pipe, from whence it passes into a water casing surrounding the smoke-box, and within the steam casing already mentioned. From here it passes into the boiler a little below the water level, at the smoke-box end. In this arrangement the movable valve in the steam-box can be regulated to discharge steam enough through the blast pipes for all ordinary purposes of draught, and also to maintain a flow of steam through the pipe beneath the boiler.

The feed water receives a large portion of the heat of this steam, from its contact with it in the casing surrounding the pipe, and, retaining the heat so obtained, it passes into the water casing in the smoke-box, where it is exposed to the heat of the waste steam on the outside, and to the temperature of the smoke-box within. It thus, when finally admitted to the boiler, has become heated quite to the boiling point, as the heat within the smoke-box of a coal engine is very great, even with long tubes. This arrangement operates as a variable exhaust by allowing any portion of the waste steam to be turned off from the blast pipes ; it effects a considerable economy in fuel by giving the water to the boiler already heated very hot; and the water casing surrounding the smoke-box prevents the destruction of the latter by the heat emitted from the tubes.

In the details of this engine the expansion valve was worked from the backing eccentric, and one lever sufficed for reversing the engine and throwing on the cut-off. This was effected by making the cut-off rocker arm work as a shell on the main valve rocker shaft, the cambs for throwing out all the hooks being on the same camb shaft, and that for the forward hook being only a quarter camb, so as to allow that hook to be on its pin in the rocker arm in two positions of the reversing lever ; that is to say, going forward with the cut-off on, and forward with it off.

The patent for the heating apparatus described, is owned by L. B. Tyng, of Lowell, who has drawings and models showing the application of the same to coal and to wood engines. For coal engines some arrangement of this nature seems obviously necessary, while for wood engines having a large extent of tube surface, with moderate length of tubes, the application of this invention appears to promise a considerable economy in fuel. The apparatus may be simplified in wood engines by pumping the water directly into a single casing about the smoke-box, and withdrawing the contact of the exhaust steam by suffering it to pass entirely up the chimney.

SECTION IV.

Details of the Locomotive Engine continued. Of the Cylinders, Steam Chests, Valves, and Steam Pipes.

THE casting for a cylinder must be perfectly sound; and this, indeed, is requisite for all the castings of a locomotive. The thickness of a cylinder, after boring, is from $\frac{3}{4}$ to $\frac{7}{8}$ inch, and about $\frac{3}{16}$ inch are taken off all around by the cutter of the boring bar. No cylinder can be truly and accurately bored in a boring lathe, unless the latter be strong and steady. The thickness of the flange of the cylinder is $1\frac{1}{4}$ inch or more. The flange by which it is secured to the frame is $1\frac{1}{2}$ inches thick, and as long as the distance between the flanges to which the cylinder heads are bolted. Four or five one-inch bolts are sufficient to secure this flange to the frame. The cylinders are generally cast separately, and are united by a bar of iron 4 by $1\frac{1}{4}$ inches, bolted to a projecting flange on each. In one or two instances we have seen them cast together, but this method makes rather an awkward casting to mould, to bore, and to fit, yet it removes the artificial connection which is otherwise necessary.

The faces of the cylinder and valve require to be ground perfectly smooth and flat, which is done by closing the ports with blocks of wood, as also the cavity in the valve; they are then ground together with fine sharp sand and water, finishing off with emery and oil. The stuffing boxes for the piston rods and valve stems require a brass lining filled with Babbitt metal. The valves are generally of cast iron, but sometimes of brass.

The valve stem in Hinkley's engines is laid in a deep recess in the upper side of the valve, and has nuts and check nuts screwed against each side of same. The valve is sometimes encircled by a wrought iron hoop or spectacle ½ inch in thickness, but increased to 1¼ inches on one side, and has the valve stem tapped into it.

The expansion valve is often worked directly on the top of the port valve. When no expansion is sought, the cut-off valve rod is placed in connection with the port valve rod, and, acquiring the motion of the latter, is relatively at rest with it. Other makers have the cut-off valve over the port valve, and in the same chest with it, but interpose a plate with valve ports between the two valves. It is, however, difficult to get at the valves where they are so placed, unless the engine has outside cylinders, or has its steam chest covers taken off from the outside. Hinkley's latest engines have covers on the side of the valve chest, which are removed from the outside of the smoke-box. But the opening on the side of the chest is no larger than to allow of taking out the valve, not being large enough to allow of setting the valves when it becomes necessary to do so, except by taking off the entire chest. In Hinkley's engines, the cut-off valve, when not required to be used, is thrown entirely off the ports, to prevent any obstruction to the passage of the steam. This is effected by an arm on the reversing camb shaft, which, when the cut-off hooks are thrown out, throws the lower rocker arm, which works the cut-off valve, entirely over, and carries the valve off its ports.

The valve seat requires to be slightly raised above the face of the casting on which it is formed, that any foreign substance received by the steam pipe may be pushed off by the valve without scratching the valve face.

Steam chests are generally of a square or oblong form, and in inside cylinder engines are enclosed within the smoke-box. In Souther's engines, however, the steam chest is round, and projects outward, so that the valve face is inclined at an angle of about 45°,—the smoke-box being made round, as a continuation of the boiler. By this arrangement he secures the advantage of a ground joint for the steam chest cover, and ready access to the valves of the engine. A ground joint is cheaper than a filed joint, and better than a putty joint. The cylinders and chests, however, from not being enclosed in the smoke-box, are exposed to the cold air, which not unfrequently, especially in winter, operates to condense the steam to an inconvenient degree. The steam chests, however, have a jacket or casing over them, and the cylinders might be lagged so as to make this a trifling objection.

The steam pipe is made of thick copper, united at one end to the vertical cast iron pipe entering the dome, and at the other end to a pipe casting formed to make a tight joint with the smoke-box sheet. The steam passes through this tee piece, and then branches off to each cylinder. All the joints about the steam pipe should be ground turning joints. Hangers of wrought iron must be made to support the steam pipe in its place. The area of the steam pipe should equal the area of two of the induction ports to the cylinder, and each branch pipe should have half this area. The exhaust pipes should have nearly the same area as the exhaust ports, until we come to the copper pipe attached as a mouth or blast pipe. This pipe at its largest place should be considerably smaller than the eduction port, and at its mouth requires to be reduced to about two inches in diameter. Most of Hinkley's

15-inch cylinder engines are running with their exhaust pipes contracted to $1\frac{7}{8}$-inch diameter at the mouth. For 16-inch cylinders, the blast pipe is 2 in. to $2\frac{1}{16}$ in. English engineers are of opinion that the fire surface of an engine should be very much increased,* in order that a proper natural draft may exist without requiring so great a reduction in the blast pipe. The resistance offered to the progress of the piston at high speeds, arising from the contraction of the blast pipes, has been stated by Stephenson, of Newcastle, to absorb one half the power of an engine. It appears to us that a large extent of heating surface, with the use of some simple expedient for regulating the draft, would produce very favorable results in the performances of locomotives. It has been proposed, instead of varying the mouth of the blast pipe, to establish a communication between the exhaust steam and the feed water of the boiler, by which means the draft could be regulated by turning off any part of the exhaust to heat the water. This plan, however, involves considerable complication, and cannot be regarded as eminently practical. We have no doubt, however, that some simple expedient will be devised for accomplishing so desirable an object.

* Dimensions of engine, by Bury, Curtis, and Kennedy, on page 36.

SECTION V.

Details of the Locomotive Engine continued. Of the Framing, Jaws, Wheels, Springs, &c.

THE framing of all the engines now built in this country is between the wheels, and rests on the bearings of the axles of the same, through the intervention of steel springs. The frames of the most recent descriptions of locomotives are solid, and have the jaws for the bearings either forged with them, or forged separately and secured to the frame by bolts. Many of these solid frames are extremely light. The most usual kind of frame, however, is the riveted frame. Two plates of flat iron, say 5 by $\frac{5}{8}$ inch, with a bar 2 inches square, riveted between them so that one of its sides is flush with the upper edges of the plates. In Hinkley's engines, and in most others, the frame passes over the bearings, and is dropped down immediately in front of the forward driving axle, to the level of the centers of the cylinders, and continues at that level to the forward end of the engine. This mode of reducing the height of the frame at the forward end, gives a ready access to the work of the machine. The jaws to this frame are of cast iron, and are secured by bolts passing up through a stout rib on the upper side of the jaw, and the 2-inch bar which is riveted in the frame. Cast iron jaws, to stand, require to be very heavy. On the "Baldwin" and "Whistler," (engines on the Lowell road, built at Lowell,) the want of strength in their jaws, which were of cast iron, and were continually breaking, made it necessary to replace them with a set of wrought iron jaws. A stout cast iron thimble is placed between the back and forward jaws; also short thimbles between the two cheeks of each jaw, and a $1\frac{1}{2}$-inch bolt is then passed through the whole, and has stout nuts at each end to secure it. Diagonal braces also pass from the ends of this bolt up to the frame, thus forming a complete truss.

Engine wheels with rims cast in sand have solid hubs. Winans' wheels with chilled rims have the hubs cast with core prints, leaving three open slots throughout their thickness. After the rim has cooled, these are filled tight with blocks of wrought iron, and the whole hub is then encircled with a strong wrought iron band. In the rims of his chilled wheels he casts a ring of wrought iron, to assist the strength of the rim; both to keep it from breaking, and to hold the rim from flying apart in case it should crack. Wrought iron tires have been exclusively used for drivers until the introduction of Winans' chilled rims, and the later method of using *chilled cast iron tires*, which were first used, we believe, by Thacher Perkins, now master of machinery on the Baltimore and Ohio Railroad. To put on a wrought tire it is first evenly heated to a moderate heat, then dropped on the rim of the wheel and quickly cooled by throwing on cold water. Seven or eight bolts with riveted heads are then passed through the tire and rim, to secure the tire from working off. To remove a tire, the bolts through the rim must be taken out, or, if rivets are used, they must be drilled out: the wheel is then laid on a circular mound of earth, a few inches high and nearly as large as the wheel; a steady but moderate heat is applied directly to the tire, the body of the wheel being covered with earth, and in a few minutes the wheel may be lifted out of the tire, by means of a crane. In this manner the tires are taken from a pair of wheels without removing them from the axle, by turning the axle up on one end so as to bring one wheel on its side.

The chilled tires, when properly cast, are better for some reasons than chilled rims; but it has not yet been satisfactorily ascertained whether either can take the place of wrought iron tires. The main difficulty anticipated in their use is an insufficient adhesion to the rails, especially in winter, when the rails are frosty or damp. The milder climate of the Southern States has prevented this from becoming so serious an objection to their adoption there. The chilled tires are three inches thick, and are bolted to the rim of the wheel. The merits of these tires above those of chilled rims, or chilled wheels, are, that if a tire breaks, it can be replaced without throwing away the wheel, and they are also readily renewed when worn out; whereas, with a chilled wheel, it is useless when the rim becomes much worn, though the rest of the wheel is perfectly sound and whole.

Chilled wheels are used almost entirely for trucks, tenders, and cars. Engine trucks are generally 30 inches in diameter, and car wheels 33 inches. Some of the roads running out of Boston have imported sets of wrought iron wheels from England, and placed them under their cars for trial. On the Boston and Providence road we have seen a pattern of cast wheel with wrought tire, and having a ring of hard wood, two inches thick, between the tire and rim of the wheel. On the above road they are placing these wheels generally under their passenger cars.

Engine trucks and car wheels are usually secured to their axles by one stout spline, and the driving wheels by two one-inch square keys.

The cranked axle is forged from a bar which is *kinked* or upset by doubling and bending so as to form the blocks for the cranks on one side of the axle. The axle is then *twisted* between the cranks till they are at right angles with each other. The crank wrist is formed by drilling out a sufficient portion of the block, left in the manufacture of the axle, and then finished by turning.

The cases for the bearings of Hinkley's engines, have dowels of a composition of equal parts of copper and tin, inserted in the case in the direction of the length of the bearing. The space between these dowels is filled with Babbitt metal. The dripper or cup has flanges to hold it in the case, and is kept in position by a screw pressing against its under side.

There is a stout spring over each driver, having one end attached by a loop to the frame, and the other to a bar between the drivers, which turns on a pin beneath the frame. The object of this bar is to equalize any effects arising from inequalities on the rail, by transmitting a portion of the shock to the wheel which is removed from this inequality. The lower end of the loop-ended rod attached to the spring, should be secured in the end of the equalizing bar by a pin, as the rod is apt to break off close to the nuts where these are used. The equalizing bar is of wrought iron, and for strength must be made deeper in the center than at the ends.

The springs are generally from 27 to 34 inches in length, and are formed of plates of $\frac{1}{4}$, $\frac{5}{16}$, or $\frac{3}{8}$ inch steel, and sometimes plates of each size. A spring of the proper form, 30 inches long, and having 14 plates of $\frac{5}{16}$, and two plates at the back of $\frac{3}{8}$ inch steel, and 3 inches wide, makes a good spring for a driver. A tit or projection is made in the end of each leaf, to fit in a punched opening in the leaf below. This is to prevent any side motion or displacement among the leaves of the spring. The end of the upper leaf is turned up to prevent the loop which passes over the end of the spring from slipping off.

Rogers, Ketchum and Grosvenor have used $\frac{1}{4}$-inch iron plates, six or eight inches long, interposed between the leaves at the middle of the spring. The leaves of the spring, when not under pressure, are in contact only at their ends; but on the application of any weight acting upon them, are brought into contact for several inches of their length. This spring, adapted to any load, is an English idea.

India-rubber springs have been applied to the driving wheels of light engines, and in many cases to the truck and tender wheels. They make, at least, a very cheap spring, and have proved well.

The iron truck frames in general use have inside bearings. They are formed of $\frac{5}{16}$-inch plates, with wrought iron bars, or thimbles, riveted between them. The side bars are made to clasp the brass boxes enclosing the bearing of the axle. A large inverted spring at each side has one end resting over the bearing of each axle, and supports the frame on its upper side. The under side of the frame is faced with a plate of steel, where it rests upon the spring. The construction of this truck does not admit of any one of the wheels rising, without raising the whole frame. Norris, and some other makers, however, make the action of the truck wheels independent of each other, by making what is called a live truck frame. In this frame the spring, instead of resting directly on the frame, rests on the bearing by a pintal passing through the frame. Any shock of the forward wheel is thus divided, and partly transmitted through the spring to the hind wheel. The Lowell Machine Shop use a truck frame, with outside bearings, on one of their patterns.

The bearings of the truck axles are from $3\frac{1}{2}$ to $3\frac{3}{4}$ inches in diameter, and $5\frac{1}{2}$ inches long. The bearings of the driving axle are from 6 to 7 inches in diameter, and 6 inches long. The crank wrists are of the same diameter as the bearings, and are 3½ to 4 inches wide. The cheeks of the cranks are 5 inches thick.

The pintal bushing for the truck is of cast iron, and is riveted between the plates forming the truck frame. The pintal is secured to the boiler behind the cylinders, or is made fast to the cylinders themselves, by being passed through the flanges connecting them together, and secured by a shoulder below and a nut above. The pintal is about 5 inches in diameter.

There should be a slide and wedge between the foot-board and tender, to prevent jarring and jolting. This wedge is drawn up in the slide by a screw and nut.

There is generally a rail, or outside frame, as it is sometimes termed, outside of the wheels. This outside frame makes a convenient support for the pump, and serves to make a walk or balcony by which to go to the forward end of the engine when it is running. This outside frame, if mounted with jaws and springs, might give additional support for the driving axle, and would assist the strength of the inside frame. The eccentrics could be placed outside the wheels, and wrought iron cranks would be keyed to the axle outside of the frame, to connect the drivers. There is no great practical difficulty, in our opinion, in keeping four bearings in line on the same axle.

It appears to us that a very light and strong tender frame could be made of flat bars 3½ by 1½ inches, and which would cost no more than our present heavily timbered wooden ones.

SECTION VI.

Details of the Locomotive Engine continued. Of the Pistons, Slides, Connecting Rods, Valve Motion, and Pumps.

THE pistons generally have two outside rings, while some makers, as Norris and others, use three. These rings are sometimes of cast iron, and sometimes of composition. The piston rings used on the Boston and Maine road are made from a composition of 80 parts copper and 20 parts tin. The outside rings are sometimes cut in four pieces, and are sometimes cut open only on one side. Cast iron rings, if not set out too tight against the inside of the cylinder, may be regarded as not only cheaper, but better than composition rings. And rings simply cut open, are better, for most reasons, than those which are cut in three or four pieces. The cover is usually secured to the body of the piston by four screws. The following are the dimensions of Hinkley's 15-inch pistons on the Maine road, and having the kind of packing-rings described as used by that road. Diam. of follower or cover, $14\frac{13}{16}$ in. ; diam. of outside rings, before cutting open, $15\frac{3}{16}$ in. ; thickness of piston, $4\frac{5}{8}$ in. ; thickness of follower, $\frac{3}{4}$ in. ; thickness of outside rings, $\frac{5}{8}$ in. ; depth of do. $1\frac{9}{16}$ in. ; inside ring of cast iron, $\frac{3}{8}$ thick. Four screws to secure cover, each one inch in diameter, 3 in. under head, and having heads $1\frac{1}{4}$ in. square. Each screw is $5\frac{5}{8}$ in. from center of piston. Four springs to set out packing, each 6 in. long, 3 in. wide, $\frac{3}{16}$ in. thick at thickest part, and having a bend or deflection of $\frac{5}{8}$ in. ;

Screws to set out packing, $\frac{5}{8}$ in. diam. Key to secure piston rod, $1\frac{3}{4}$ by $\frac{1}{16}$. Thickness of iron around rod, $1\frac{3}{4}$ in.; diam. of body of iron penetrated by screws to secure cover, is 2 in., and is connected to the hub of the piston head by a bridge of iron $\frac{7}{8}$ in. thick.

Winans' 17-inch piston has six screws to secure the cover, and each spring which is set out by the packing screws, presses at each end against the center of a smaller spring, thus making 24 bearings against the packing rings.

All this is unnecessary, and makes the springs liable to derangement. Norris' springs are 9 inches long, there being three in his 14-inch piston.

The best slides are undoubtedly the flat slides first used in the old Locks and Canals Co.'s Engines. These are now used by Rogers and others. The simplest and cheapest form of slide is the round slide used by Norris, and until recently by Hinkley. The length of cross-head bearing on the slides is generally 10 or 12 inches. The diameter of the round slides is $2\frac{1}{4}$ in. One end of the slides is attached to lugs on the cylinder cover, the other to a wrought iron loop supported by a cross girt under the boiler.

The connecting rods have oval or octagonal boxes on the outward sides of the bearings, and square boxes on the inner sides, or where they abut against the end of the rod. The straps are generally 1 in. to $1\frac{1}{4}$ in. thick, and in width $2\frac{1}{2}$ in. at the crank end, and $2\frac{1}{4}$ in. at the cross-head end. The straps are secured by two $\frac{7}{8}$ in. bolts to each, and the boxes are set up by a key generally $1\frac{3}{4}$ and $\frac{3}{4}$ inch wide and $\frac{5}{8}$ thick at the crank end, and by a somewhat smaller key at the cross-head end. The most recent method of securing the key in its place is to have its smaller end pass through a piece of iron, on the outside of the strap, and an inch thick; this piece being secured to the strap by one of the bolts already noticed. A set screw in this piece pinches the end of the key, while another screw at the center of the flat face of the rod is turned against the key at that point. The rod is generally not far from six feet between the centers, and is nearly or quite 3 inches in diameter at the center. The cross-head bearing, when of cast iron, is 2¾ inches in diameter.

As the boxes in the connecting rod become worn, the setting them up by the keys tends to lengthen the rod, as the outside boxes retain their places, while the inside boxes are moved outward. In the main connecting rod this is no great evil, as there is generally sufficient allowance at the end of the cylinder for the piston to work up a little without hitting the head, and for this purpose there should be more clearance given at the forward end of the cylinder than at the hind end; say, on a new engine, ¼ in. allowance at the hind end, and nearly ½ inch on the forward end. On the rods, however, to connect the drivers together, it is essential that the original length of the rod be constantly preserved; and to do this, the key at one end of the rod presses the inner box outward, while the other key, being outside the box at that end of the rod, presses the outer box inwards. On Winans' and on Perkins' engines, having four pairs of wheels to connect, the bearing is bored out of the end of the rod, a tight bushing inserted, and no keys used.

The valve motion generally used is the indirect attachment of the eccentric, through the rocker shaft. In ordinary inside cylinder engines, a shaft 1¾ in. in diam. is secured by stands to the cross girt supporting the slides. On this shaft there are two wrought iron tubes or shells, one for receiving and communicating the motion for each valve. The thickness of these tubes is ⅝ inch. The rocker arms which support the hooks are 6½ inches between the centers, their hubs ⅝ to $\frac{3}{4}$ inch thick, and the arms are $\frac{3}{4}$ inch thick. The pins or bolts which support the hooks have thimbles $1\frac{1}{4}$ in. diameter, and $\frac{3}{16}$ in. thick. The rocker shaft, tubes, arms, and thimbles, are all of wrought iron. (In some instances cast iron tubes, with the arms cast therewith, have been used, and when working on a wrought iron shaft, have less friction than the wrought iron tubes. The Taunton Co. have used cast iron rocker tubes on upwards of sixty engines, without breakage.) The pin for the valve stem is turned with a shoulder, and is passed through the end of the upper arm, and secured by a nut on the back side of same. The thickness of the upper arm is $1\frac{1}{4}$ to $1\frac{1}{2}$ inches, and is of the same length as the lower arm. The arms on the rocker shaft, which receive the motion of the hand hooks, are 10 inches between the centers. The object of the hand hooks is to catch the eccentric hooks when the engine is reversed, and also to assist in starting in difficult situations, as in a drift of snow. The inside of the eccentric hooks, where they wear on the thimbles of the rocker arms, are faced with a wedge or dowel of hardened steel. The eccentric rods are $1\frac{1}{2}$ to $1\frac{3}{4}$ inches in diameter, and have right and left nuts to adjust their length. The end of the rod is secured to the brass hoop or eccentric band by bolts, or by being passed through a hub formed on same, with nuts and check nuts on each side. The eccentric band is $1\frac{1}{4}$ inches thick, and is lined with Babbitt metal. The eccentrics generally have three inches throw, and in inside cylinder engines, must be cast in two pieces to allow of their being placed between the cranks. The eccentrics are secured to the axle by set screws turned at their ends to a blunt point, and entering the axle. This is to give a chance for altering the lead of the valve when required, which could not be so readily done were the eccentrics keyed to the axle. It is for this reason, also, that the eccentrics are generally cast separately, although some engines have the four eccentrics for forward and backward motion for each valve cast in one piece, or at least in two pieces, to put together around the axle. The strap under the hook is $\frac{1}{2}$ to $\frac{5}{8}$ thick, and long enough that the hook may traverse, when thrown out, in either direction, without striking the thimble in the rocker arms. The cambs for raising the hooks are of cast iron, and have a throw of 2 inches or more. These cambs are secured to a wrought iron shaft $1\frac{1}{2}$ to $1\frac{3}{4}$ inches in diameter, having a pinion of 12 or 14 teeth on one end and turned by a segment, which is worked by the reversing lever on the footboard.

The expansion valve is worked through the medium of a separate rocker shaft, having also a camb shaft, with reversing rod to work the same. As this camb shaft requires to be turned but one quarter around, a simple arm attached to it is all that is necessary.

The hooks are sometimes formed with V-shaped openings, in order that they may readily catch the pins when reversed.

This general arrangement of operating the valve has been recently superseded in a measure by the introduction of Stephenson's link motion, although the old establishments still adhere to the use of the rocker shaft. An open curved link is attached at one extremity to the forward rod, and at the other to the backing rod from the eccentrics. A block attached to the valve stem is made to fit this link, while the link can be raised or lowered so as to bring this block within the action of either rod. By this method, whenever the engine is reversed, the ports are ready to take steam, as the act of raising or lowering the link moves the valve to its proper position on the face of the cylinder. As this method of working the valve admits of giving it a variable throw, advantage is sometimes taken of this circumstance to work expansively. Indeed, it was for this purpose that Stephenson first secured a patent (in England,) for its use. The valve, however, should generally have a determinate throw, depending on the size of the ports which it covers; and any increase or diminution of this throw is attended with a choking of the induction and eduction of the steam. This result may be made evident by making a section of the steam ports on the side of a small piece of board having its edges straight, and making a section of the valve on another straight piece of wood. If the edges of these boards are applied to each other, it will be seen that any other travel than between 2½ and 3½ inches, would not readily allow of the proper passage of the steam. The travel of the valve, for this reason, is generally fixed at 3 inches.

A modification of the link motion, without altering, however, its essential features, was devised by Sharp, Brothers & Co., of Manchester, England, and applied to the goods engines constructed by them for the Great Western Line. The link was curved the opposite way to Stephenson's, his link being described from the center of the axle, and was suspended by a straight link to the boiler or frame. The eccentric rods thus retaining one position, the block was attached to the valve stem by a jointed arm, and was raised or lowered by a lever for that purpose. There are more joints about this arrangement than in Stephenson's, and its only merit above Stephenson's is that the jointed valve stem may be raised with less power than the whole weight of the eccentric rods and links. The use of this motion for obtaining a variable expansion, is of course liable to the same objections as Stephenson's.

A form of variable cut-off, introduced by Horace

Gray, Esq., of Boston, upon the Fitchburg, New York and Erie, and other roads, consists in an open curved link formed as an arm on the upper side of the cut-off rocker shaft. The cut-off valve rod being jointed near the stuffing-box, and attached to a block in this link, can be raised or lowered to acquire any throw within the limits of motion of the block. By this method a variable expansion is obtained without affecting the induction or eduction of steam in the cylinder.

To set the valves of a locomotive, the piston is brought to the end of its stroke, the valve is placed over the ports so as to have the desired lead or advance on the piston; the eccentric rods are then adjusted to such a length as to allow the hooks to catch the pins, the valve retaining the position previously given. The engine is now moved either forward or backward, as may be convenient, until the piston is brought to the other extreme of its stroke; and if the valve has the same advance on the second port as on the first, it is properly set. If, however, the lead is more or less than that given to the first port to which the valve was set, the eccentrics require to be turned in the proper direction on the axle, and to such an extent as to give the desired lead. Before turning the eccentrics, the eccentric rod must be lengthened or shortened, as the case may require, so as to divide the difference of lead on the two ports, in order that it may be equal on each. A proper adjustment of the length of the rods makes the lead *equal* on each extreme of the stroke, while the position given to the eccentrics determines the *amount* of lead.

The eccentrics may be properly fixed to the crank axle, when it is detached from the wheels and from the engine.

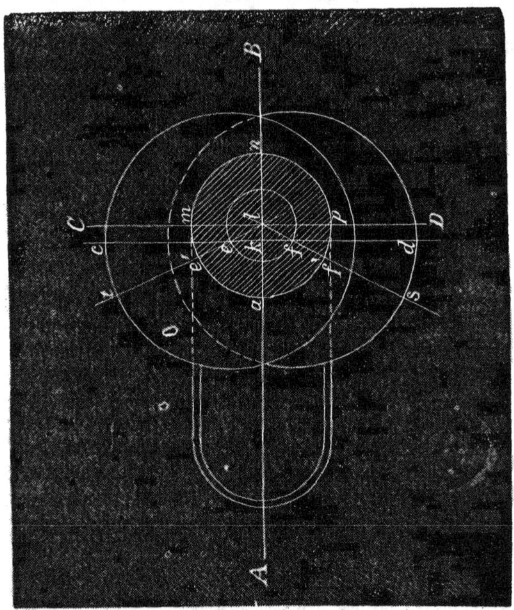

Cylinder side.

Find the point a on the side of the axle, and in the horizontal line, A, B, connecting the centers of the crank. Then take a piece of tin or sheet iron and describe on it the circle a, m, n, p, of the size of the axle; from the same center describe a circle equal to the throw of the valve. Then if the valve has an indirect attachment, as in case of the rocker shaft, lay off on the cylinder side of the axle, the crank being turned that way, a distance, k, l, equal to the sum of the lap and lead at one end of the valve; draw *c*, *d*, through the point *k*, and perpendicular to the line *A*, *B*. Through the points *e* and *f*, where this line intersects the circle described by the throw of the eccentric, draw the diagonal lines *l*, *t*, and *l*, *s*, passing through the points *e* and *f*, and the center of the axle. The points e' and f', at which these diagonals intersect the circumference of the axle, may be transferred by the compasses to the axle from the point *a* already found on its side. The extremity of the line dividing the forward eccentric in two equal parts, will fall on e', and the line dividing the backward eccentric will fall on f', as will be seen by the diagram.

In setting valves with direct attachment, the distance, *k*, *l*, is applied to the other side of the center of the axle, and the diagonal lines tend the other way.

We have already explained the nature of lead, and we should perhaps have explained the term *lap* before entering upon the foregoing instructions for setting valves. When the valve is in the middle of its travel or motion on the face of the cylinder, the distance which it laps at each end over the induction ports, is called the lap of the valve. The effect of this lap is to shut off the steam before the piston has completed its stroke, and the lap valve thus acts as an expansion valve, to a greater or less extent as the lap is more or less considerable. Indeed, the main difficulty in the use of a lap valve for a cut-off, is that of starting, especially with a heavy load or on a bad grade. Engines having no separate cut-off valves usually have as much lap to the valves as will admit the steam to the cylinders without serious difficulty in starting. The effect of combined lead and lap, when restricted within proper limits, is to augment the speed of the engine; the *lead*, by assisting the change in the motion of the piston so as to lose no time, and the *lap* to act as a cut-off valve, to derive the benefits resulting from an expansion of the steam. These benefits, as we shall hereafter demonstrate, consist in being able to do more work with the same steam, from which result a considerable economy in fuel, and a diminution in the water carried in the boiler.

The pumps of an engine are either attached directly to the cross-head, and have the same stroke as the piston, or they are worked by the same through a lever proportioned so as to give the pump plunger one-half or one-third the stroke of the piston. Many recent engines, however, including Hinkley's patterns, have an arm attached to the outside crank pin, which communicates motion to the hind pair of drivers, the end of this arm being brought up to within $3\frac{3}{4}$ inches from the center of the wheel, and working the pump plunger, giving it a stroke of $7\frac{1}{2}$ inches. The pumps, when this connection is used, are placed at the hind end of the outside framing, and beneath the footboard. The feed water enters the boiler on the side of the fire-box at a point about as high as the lower row of tubes. Some contend that the feed water should be injected at the bottom of the water space about the fire-box, or at the smoke-box end of the boiler, in order that the cooling effects of the water may not act directly upon the tube sheets, and by alternately contracting and expanding them, cause the tubes to leak.

Pumps having one-half or one-third stroke are generally better for engines running quick, than full stroke pumps, as the barrel of the pump is more sure to fill, while the wear of the valves is not so perceptible.

The pumps on all recent engines are provided with air vessels of iron or brass. The form of cup valve working in a brass cage, used by Souther, appears to us the simplest form of valve which can be devised. It requires much less fitting than any other form of valve which we remember to have seen.

The joints between the pump and the suction and air chambers, and the joint in the check valve chamber, are usually ground joints of cast iron. These, however, when long in use, frequently become leaky, as a cast iron joint about a pump, or in any place where the water has access to it, is found not to hold its *face* well. If a composition ring be placed inside the valve chamber, to make a joint upon, the iron with which it is in contact becomes subject to a peculiar oxidation, arising from a kind of galvanic action with the composition ring. The iron about this ring often becomes *eat* full of small holes. To remedy this evil the pumps of Souther's engines have rings of a composition *cast* inside the valve chambers, and in every situation about the pump where a ground joint is required. These rings are first cast by themselves, and their composition is so proportioned that when placed in the mould of the valve chambers, and having the melted iron poured around them, the iron just melts the surface of the ring, and thereby becomes firmly cast with it, so that water, which is necessary for the galvanic action described, cannot enter between them. We regard this as a very excellent plan, as it saves much expense in keeping the pumps in order, and makes no material difference in the first cost of the pump.

The keys to tighten the bearings about an engine should not have too much taper, as there is danger of their becoming set so tight as to cause the melting of the Babbitt lining of the boxes. When much tapered, they are also liable to work out, but this does not prevent them from being set so tight as to create the mischief referred to. All the bolts should be turned and fitted, and for such as pass through the straps of the connecting rods, and other parts in motion, check nuts are required. The thread of the screws should not be too coarse, as in that case the nuts are apt to work off, while if too fine, the thread is liable to strip. A thread of eleven to the inch appears to answer very well for the medium-sized bolts.

Such rubbing surfaces about an engine as are liable to become rapidly worn, require a lining of the composition usually named Babbitt metal, from the inventor, Mr. Isaac Babbitt, of Boston. A space is left around the inside of the shell of the bearing, which is filled with this composition, there being ledges around the sides of the shell to keep the soft metal from coming out. A common proportion for the ingredients of this composition is twenty parts tin, two of antimony, and one of copper.

There should always be oil cups on the cross-heads and means must be found to oil every rubbing surface about the engine.

There should be a little chance for end playon the pins for the connecting rod to connect the drivers, and also on the pins for the pump rod. This play on the connecting rod may amount to ¼ inch, and is necessary to allow the wheels to ride freely around a curve.

We shall have occasion to mention two or three particular patterns of engines, and in so doing shall notice some peculiar arrangements in the various parts of their moving machinery, differing from what we have described. A disposition is constantly shown among makers for improvements, and new applications possessing their peculiar advantages and disadvantages are constantly appearing. Our most recent engines possess many decided improvements over those constructed but a very few years ago.

SECTION VII.

Remarks on the Management of Engines.

A well-built engine, having its parts easily accessible, and possessing good qualities for the production of steam, may, with careful management, be made to run for a long time with but little expense for repairs. The points to which the careful engineman directs his attention, are the manner of firing, the supply of feed water, the proper adaptation of the production of steam to the features of the road, and various other particulars of a like nature, which are necessary for the proper performance of a locomotive. It is, of course, necessary to fire up oftener when the engine is performing hard work, than when the load is light. The fire should be maintained at a proper point to make sufficient steam, and should not be suffered to get so low as to affect the pressure in the boiler. It is an object, however, in approaching a terminal station, to have barely sufficient fire to reach the engine house. The supply of feed water to the boiler is regulated very much by local circumstances on the road. In ascending grades, the injection of cold water would check the formation of steam, and it is therefore necessary to have a good supply of water in the boiler before reaching the foot of an unfavorable grade. On long levels and on descending grades, one pump may be kept working to nearly its full extent. It is seldom that both pumps require to be at work at the same time. There should also be plenty of water in the boiler before reaching either roadside or terminal stations. The fire door should be kept open as little as possible, as the entrance of the cold air through it contracts the tube sheets, and is sometimes the cause of their leaking.

If an engine has a variable exhaust, it is a good plan to open it to nearly its full extent, when firing, and to immediately contract it very much, so as to recover the fire quickly. The cylinders and valves require to be oiled at every fifteen or twenty miles of the journey. Melted tallow is used for this purpose. If the ports of the throttle valve are of the same area as the steam pipe, it is found best to keep the throttle partly closed, as when the pressure in the steam pipe is rather less than in the boilers, the engine is not so liable to prime. The proper opening for the throttle of any engine can soon be determined from observation.

In going through covered bridges and station-houses, enginemen are generally cautioned to shut their dampers, and to otherwise check the draft of their engines, so as to guard against fire.

The boiler requires to be blown off at intervals of a week or more. The times at which this operation should be performed will depend very much on the purity of the water used. When a scale deposits on the tubes, and on the internal shell of the boiler, a double handful of mahogany sawdust thrown in at the safety valve will tend to remove it.

There should be as few putty joints about an engine as possible; but where there are any joints requiring packing, putty seems to answer better than India-rubber. It should be mixed to have a very firm and even consistency, which end is best attained by mixing the red and white lead of which it is composed by beating with a heavy hand-hammer.

The hemp for packing the piston rods, valve stems, and pump plungers, should be soaked in warm water before using. Some engineers soak it in melted tallow, but this appears to rot it. Hemp simply soaked in warm water will be found strong after two months' use. Good hemp is to be preferred to India-rubber for stuffing boxes.

The frequent use of the sand-box on freight engines has the effect of rapidly wearing out the tires of the wheels. Its use should therefore be restricted to cases where it cannot be dispensed with.

In repainting the wood work about an engine, the best way of cleaning the work from grease and dirt is to wet it with spirits of turpentine on a handful of waste. The steam chimneys are best polished with rotten-stone, used with oil on a woollen cloth.

Every engine man should know whether the spring balances of his safety valves are correctly marked. To test the balances themselves, they can be attached to a balance known to be correct, and if the weight indicated on each balance is the same, the spring of your engine balance is correct. If you wish to find whether the spring balance is correctly marked, — say, for instance, to a pressure of 90 lbs. to the inch, — find in the first place the diameter of the valve seat, or smallest diameter of the valve, and find its corresponding area in square inches. Multiply this area by 90, and you have the entire pressure against the whole valve. Now from this pressure deduct the weight of the safety valve lever, with the spring balance attached and disconnected from the boiler, the lever being weighed at a point directly over the center of the safety valve. What remains is the pressure against the valve, which is to be overcome by the tension of the spring balance, unaided by its weight. Multiply this pressure by the distance in inches from the center of the joint pin or fulcrum, to the center of the valve pin, and divide the product by the distance from the joint pin to the center of the spring balance. This quotient shows the tension of the spring balance, requisite to overcome a pressure of 90 lbs. per square inch against the valve. Suppose this quotient to be 81, for instance; then in re-marking the spring balance, the point showing 90 lbs. per inch should be at 81, as originally marked by the maker of the spring balance on his scale. If the original marks of the spring balance have been covered or destroyed, then attach a weight equal to the quotient found in the above calculation, and the point to which it draws down the gauge or pointer may be marked, and calculated from as though it were the original mark.

If the balance be screwed down to any point supposed to show a certain pressure in the boiler, a pair of steelyards can be applied to the *end* of the safety valve lever, when the spring balance is screwed to that pressure and is attached to the boiler, and the resistance or tension of the balance, or the weight sufficient to just raise it, may be noted. This weight may be multiplied by the distance from the joint pin to the balance, and the product divided by the distance from the joint pin to the center of the valve; the quotient will be the pressure against the valve, which if divided by the number of square inches in the area of the valve, will show the pressure per inch. This method, it will be seen, gives the true result also without deducting the weight of the lever in the calculation, as its weight is included in getting the tension of the spring balance.

No careful engineman puts out his fires by throwing water in the fire-box, except in cases demanding the immediate withdrawal of the fire. It is even then better to pull out the grate bars by a dart, which can be done if the fire-box be not full of wood, as the injury caused by contracting the tube sheets is irreparable. To reverse the steam also when the engine is in motion brings a very powerful strain upon its bearings. It should never be done, except to prevent collision or running off the track. When, to prevent a collision, it sometimes becomes necessary, however, to reverse full steam ahead to full steam back, a difficulty is sometimes found in catching the hooks. The hand hooks, too, when dropped on the pins, do not immediately catch, until they will suddenly become engaged and put the hand levers in rapid motion, so as to become a source of danger to the engineman. It is best, therefore, in reversing in such cases, to place the reversing lever first midway, with all the eccentric hooks out, when the hand hooks may be at once caught and the back hooks immediately thrown in. We know old engineers who say they always do this in cases of the most imminent danger, and on the whole it generally takes less time. Where an engine has V-hooks, or links, there is never any difficulty in reversing at once.

In removing and replacing the steam chest and cylinder covers, care should be taken that no one screw which secures them shall be up to a tight bearing when the others are loose. In putting them on, the nuts should be turned loosely up all around, and then gradually tightened. Unless these precautions are observed there is danger of cracking the covers.

There are very few roads where any account is kept of the work performed by their locomotives, so as to show the comparative power of each engine on the road. Every new engine is, to a certain extent, an experiment, and its performance will very much depend on some of the details observed in its construction. An engineman knowing the features of the road over which he runs, as the radii of the curves, length and height of grades, &c., may keep a very useful and interesting abstract of the load drawn, or speed attained, together with the consumption of fuel, oil, &c., on some of the trips performed by the machine in his charge. These particulars are practically useful, inasmuch as they show what may be expected of a locomotive under ordinary circumstances; and they also facilitate comparisons of the different patterns of engines. Some of the roads running out of Boston keep a monthly list posted in their engine-houses, of the number of miles run by each of their engines, together with the amount of oil and waste used for the same time.

The following is an estimate which has been furnished us of the expenses for running a first class passenger engine, 100 miles a day for one year.

Wages of Engineman, - - -	$720.00
" " Fireman, - - - - -	360.00
Wood: 4 cords per day, 280 days 1120 cords @ $4.50 per cord, -	5,040.00
Oil; 280 gallons, @ .80 - -	224.00
Waste; 840 lbs., " .02 - -	16.80
Repairs; 28000 miles, " .06 - -	1,680.00
Water in Boston, - - - - -	100.00
Water and pumping on road, - -	150.00
Interest on first cost of engine, - -	480.00
Total,	$8,770.80

This, though but an approximation, serves to show pretty nearly the general expense of locomotive power.

In our railroad reports generally, no mention is made of the details of the expenditures on account of the locomotive department, and while the entire success of the road depends upon the condition of this branch of its fixtures, the subject is passed without the least notice. Those interested in railroad matters may regard the locomotive of the present day as practically perfect; this, however, would be a serious error, and would very much retard the introduction of beneficial improvements. On some of the Southern roads, the Baltimore and Ohio, for instance, a detailed account is appended to the superintendent's yearly report, containing the number, names, rank, classes, and builders of all the engines on the road; their performances for the preceding year in miles run, expense for repairs on each engine, together with details of the charges for fuel, wages, oil, waste, and incidental expenses connected therewith.

The Baltimore and Ohio Railroad* is one of the largest enterprises of the kind in the country. Its entire length from Baltimore to Cumberland, including the branch to the City of Washington, is 220 miles; and there are by the last returns sixty-three locomotives on the road. The careful attention paid to the minutæ of the running department on that road presents a model which our engineers might well follow.

* This Company are now extending their road to Wheeling, making the entire road, when finished, 431 miles long. The difficult passage over the Alleghany Mountains will present some of the boldest and most striking works of art to be seen in this country. The new tunnel to pass through the mountain ridge will be one mile and one quarter long. Several iron bridges of 180 feet span; also stone masonry bridges of that span will be erected to carry the line across the numerous mountain streams. This extension will greatly increase the already immense traffic now finding its channel in the Baltimore and Ohio Road.

SECTION VIII.

Various Patterns of Locomotives.

The most recent patterns of passenger engines have 15-inch inside cylinders, four 5-feet or 5 ½-feet drivers, and a truck frame. This general arrangement is seldom modified to any material extent, although the diameter of cylinder is made by Norris 13 inches, and in some instances, by other makers, 16 inches. The use of two pairs of drivers is necessary to obtain sufficient adhesion to the rails, although an engine having but one pair of drivers runs much easier, and is to be preferred for special trains of a few cars, and running only for short distances over a nearly level track.

For freight transportation the cylinder is generally 16 to 18 inches in diameter, and the driving wheels from 42 to 54 inches in diameter. Hinkley and Norris have each patterns of ten-wheel engines, with six drivers connected, and Winans' freight engines have eight wheels connected and supporting the entire weight of the engine.

Within a year or two there have been constructed several engines in various parts of the country, of novel and peculiar design. The chief feature, however, in these engines has been an increase in the size of the driving wheels. Among these engines was one built by Edward S. Norris, of Schenectady, N. Y., for the Utica and Schenectady Railroad, of the following dimensions:

Sixteen-inch cylinder, 22-inch stroke; boiler 42 inches in diameter; 116 two-inch tubes, 10 ft., 3 in. long; grate about 14 square feet; one pair of wrought iron driving wheels behind the fire-box, and 7 feet in diameter; one pair of wrought iron bearing wheels just forward of the fire-box, and 4 feet in diameter, and a truck frame beneath the smoke-box of four 3½-feet wrought iron wheels. The cylinders are outside, and are placed in a horizontal position midway between the fire and smoke boxes. A large dome, at a corresponding point on the top of the boiler, supplies steam to the cylinders through pipes running down outside the boiler to the steam chests. The valve motion is the modified form of Stephenson's link motion, on which we have remarked on a preceding page. The frame of the engine is below the axle of the driving wheels, and above that of the 4-feet bearing wheels, the jaws for the bearings of the driving axle being formed on the upper side of the frame. There is also an outside frame having a floating bearing for the end of the driving axle, the crank and eccentrics being between this bearing and the wheel.

The performance of this engine is represented as being remarkably good.

The coal-burning engine, built by Ross Winans, of Baltimore, and placed by him for trial on the Boston and Maine Railroad, had 17-inch outside cylinders laid horizontally, 22-inch stroke, and eight drivers, having chilled rims 43 inches in diameter, all the drivers being placed between the fire and smoke boxes. The connecting rod is applied to the third pair of wheels from the smoke-box. The distance between the centers of the extreme axle is 11 ft., 3 in.; between the centers of the cylinders, 6 ft., 5 in. The boiler shell is made of $\frac{5}{16}$ iron, and measures, in its smallest inside diameter, 41 inches. There are 101 two-and-one-half-inch, and 2 two-inch wrought iron tubes, 13 feet in length. The upper row of tubes is nearly up to the top of the cylinder part of the boiler, the water-level being in the dome above the waist of the boiler. The dome is formed a little forward of the middle point of the boiler, having the same diameter, and rising 51 inches above it. There is a step on the back side of the fire-box, making the length of the grate 14 inches more than the length of the crown sheet. The fire-box is of ⅜ inch copper, with the exception of the tube sheet, which is of ½ inch iron. Length of grate, 56½ in.; at crown sheet, 42½ in.; mean breadth of grate, 42½ in.; at center of boiler or middle row of tubes, 39½ in.; all inside measures. The whole depth from the crown sheet to grate is 51½ inches. The grate bars are very heavy, and are cast but two together. Their ends come through the bottom of the fire-box, on the back side, and have round holes through which to put a bar to stir them occasionally, in order to loosen the cinders and melted coal. The exhaust from both cylinders comes through a cast iron box or blast pipe having movable sides, so that the aperture at its mouth may be varied from 3¼ to 10 square inches. There is a pipe about 9 inches in diameter, passing up through the smoke-box, from the bottom to the top, and entering the chimney, leaving a few inches all around it for the smoke to rise through. The exhaust enters this pipe at its bottom, and the partial vacuum created by its action supplies the blast, as in ordinary locomotives. The tube surface of this engine is 860 square feet; of heating surface in fire-box, 66 square feet; and the area of grate is 16⅔ square feet.

Messrs. Slade and Currier, civil engineers, were commissioned to make experiments with this engine, in order to institute a comparison between it and a first-class wood engine, but more particularly to test its actual value as a coal-burning engine. The results of their experiments have been published, but they neglect to state that the "New Hampshire," (the wood engine,) was of a materially different pattern from the "coaler," inasmuch as it had six driving wheels and a truck frame, thereby losing a considerable per cent. of the adhesion due to its weight as compared with the "coaler." The dimensions of the "New Hampshire" were as follows: 16-inch cylinder, 20-inch stroke; diameter of drivers, 46 inches; length of tubes, 10 ft., 6 in.; diameter of boiler, 45 inches. This engine was built by Hinkley & Drury.

The experimental trips were made in the latter part of January and in the beginning of February, 1850. The entire distance from Boston to Great Falls is given as 74 miles. There was more or less snow on the track during the time in which the experiments were made. The highest grades were about 47 feet per mile. One point unfavorable for the "coaler" was the fact that from there being but about 26 miles of double track, the freight trains were subject to frequent and protracted delays, in waiting for passenger trains to pass. In waiting, the fire in the wood engine could be suffered to go nearly down, the fire-box being filled with wood when the train came in sight. In the coal engine, however, it was necessary to keep the furnace filled with coal, as, if suffered to get down, it would take considerable time to recover the fire.

With the "coaler," the average of ten trips showed a consumption of 4786 lbs. anthracite coal to evaporate 3512 gallons in going 74 miles; this being 10.31 lbs. coal required to evaporate one cubic foot of water.

With the wood engine, 3 cords and $\frac{4}{10}$ of a foot of wood of various qualities and prices were used to evaporate 3734 gallons of water.

The cost of carrying 15000 tons one mile with wood was found to be, - - - - - - $14.04
With coal, - - - - - - - 12.70

Favor of coal, - - - - - - $1.34

The wood engine had a sand-box, and had wrought iron tires: the "coaler" had a sand-box, also, but had chilled wheels.

The "coaler" took 76 cars, weighing, with freight, 433 tons, up Ward Hill, in Bradford, where there is a grade of 47 feet per mile, and also a very bad reversed curve. In going up the hill no sand was used, nor did the wheels slip, except, as the report states, some three or four turns where some track repairers had taken off a hand car and left a little snow on the rails.

The wood engine took 61 cars up the same hill, weighing, with freight, 391 tons. Sand was constantly running from the sand-box, except when, to ascertain whether the engine was working up to its full power, the sand was turned off, when the wheels were found to slip very much.

The average cost of wood used on the through trips was $3.63 per cord.

The cost of anthracite coal, per ton of 2240 pounds, was $5.25; $\frac{5}{8}$ of a ton of coal was found to be equal in effect for evaporation to one cord of wood, or $3.28 worth of coal equal to $3.63 worth of wood.

The average speed of the coaler, although having a smaller wheel and a longer stroke, was found to be $\frac{2}{10}$ of a mile per hour greater than that of the wood engine. Their average speeds being $14\frac{3}{10}$ and $14\frac{1}{10}$ miles per hour, respectively. This was probably owing to a loss on the wood engine by slipping the wheels.

In conclusion, the commissioners express their opinion that, for runinng heavy trains, which are not obliged to wait for any considerable length of time along the line, for other trains to pass, they believe coal to be every way more economical than wood. They also say that in their remarks they would not wish to be considered as in any way disparaging the "New Hampshire," as they consider that a first class wood engine.

Winans has an express engine on the Worcester road, having 7-feet drivers. In this engine, however, the proportions of the boiler, &c., are very much the same as in the freight engine we have noticed. These seven feet drivers were cast with chilled rims, and were of an extremely light pattern; in fact, they became broken before they had been used two months. There were two small steam cylinders placed on the sides of the boiler over the bearings of the driving axle, by which the weight on the drivers could be varied from three to twelve and a half tons. But when under their utmost adhesion, the drivers were found to slip very much.

Many attempts have been made to burn anthracite coal effectually and economically. Winans' engines appear the best adapted for the use of this kind of fuel of any yet constructed. We regard, however, a very large extent of grate with a moderate depth of coal as still more likely to attain to superior results. For a 17-inch cylinder, let the grate be 6 feet by $3\frac{1}{2}$ feet, the depth of fire-box being 3 feet, and having two or three water bridges 4 inches in thickness traversing its entire length. We are of opinion that anthracite might be burned in such a fire-box with increased effect in the production of steam, and with a diminished waste in the metal of the fire-box and grate bars. With such a furnace, a pair of small wheels would be necessary to support the hind end of it.

The difficulties encountered in the use of hard coal arise chiefly from the intense and concentrated heat involved in its combustion, thereby destroying the grate bars and *scaling* the inside of the fire-box. This rapid burning out of the grate has led to leaving off the ash pan on the coal engines on some of the Pennsylvania roads, which appears to remove to some extent the destructive results attending the use of the coal. The ashes and cinders falling upon the track, if they do not *immediately* cause a fire, which must be guarded against, soon form an impenetrable crust along the entire line, which removes all further danger from that source. This, though it may appear somewhat improbable at the first view, accords with the experience of the roads where it has been tried. Much difficulty has been met in the use of copper tubes, as the action of the coal, from being projected in small pieces by the blast, was found to cut them away near their mouths. This difficulty suggested the use of wrought iron tubes, which, however, require much caution in setting them, as the increased force necessary to head up their ends is apt to spring or bend the tube sheet. A method has been practised with much success on the Pennsylvania roads, which is to turn off an inch or more of the end of the wrought iron tube in the form of the frustum of a cone, thereby reducing its thickness one half at its extreme end. The tube is then placed through the tube sheet, and a thin thimble of copper, an inch in length, and previously turned off in the same manner as the tubes, is driven into the mouth of the tube, with its sharpest edge foremost. After being driven as far as it will go, the thick edge projecting outwards is turned over and headed in the usual manner.

The creation of sufficient blast by the action of the exhaust steam has also been attended with some difficulty. Anthracite requires for its proper combustion a very steady and quite powerful blast, which the intermittent and fitful action of the blast pipe of a locomotive fails of producing. It has been attempted by many arrangements, however, to render this kind of blast regular and capable of giving the required intensity to the fire.

The pipe described as passing up through the smoke-box of Winans' engine, has this result for its object. Although the steam enters the bottom of this pipe by sudden and violent impulses, the pipe must be filled with steam, which will issue in a very regular manner from the top of it, where its action is first employed in causing a draft through the tubes. It has also been tried to obtain a regular blast by letting the exhaust steam into a receiver or box a foot in diameter and a foot high, this box being in the middle of the smoke-box. Eighteen one-inch tubes in the top of this box afforded exit for the steam. This plan, however, from the resistance caused by the steam on the reverse side of the piston (being solicited to escape through so difficult a passage,) has rendered its operation inefficient.

If future experience determines the exhaust steam to be insufficient to give a proper blast for burning anthracite, it will become necessary to adopt some of the varieties of bituminous coals, or a mixture of anthracite and bituminous coal. We think, however, the exhaust steam will be found sufficient for burning the former, under ordinary circumstances, with a large extent of fire-box surface.

We will now notice a few other patterns of engines from which our remarks on burning coal have arrested our attention.

The "John Stevens," by Norris, Brothers, of Philadelphia, had 13-inch cylinders, 34-inch stroke, and one pair of eight feet drivers. This engine was intended to burn coal. Its operation, however, was not attended with the anticipated results.

O. W. Bayley, of the Amoskeag Machine Shop, at Manchester, N. H., has lately built an engine with 15-inch cylinders, 24-inch stroke, and two pairs of seven feet drivers. There were two stout shafts, resting in bearings beneath the frame, and between the cylinders and driving axle. Each of these shafts had two stout arms keyed to it, the one in a line with the piston rod, to which its upper extremity was attached by a link; the other outside the frame, and which, by the connecting rod attached to it, communicated motion to the driving wheels. The use of this arrangement was to obtain the supposed advantages of inside cylinders with an outside connection. If the proposed object was to reduce the height of the boiler from the rails by avoiding the use of the crank axle, we think it might have been better attained through the use of outside cylinders, placed midway on the boiler, and connected to the hind pair of drivers. It could not be supposed that the use of inside cylinders would contribute to give the engine a steady motion on the road, so long as the power was applied outside the wheels. Had the cylinders been placed as near as they could set to the forward pair of wheels and clear them, it would have been merely necessary to let the valve stems enter the steam chests on the front side.

G. S. Griggs has lately finished an engine for the Providence road of the following general particulars: — 14¾-inch cylinders; 18-inch stroke; about a 44-inch boiler; 9½-feet tubes; six driving wheels, supporting the entire weight of the engine, and being 48 inches in diameter. These wheels had chilled rims, and were all cast with flanges. One pair of wheels was behind the fire-box, and the connecting rod was applied to the middle pair of wheels. From the center of the hind pair of wheels to the center of the middle pair, was 5 feet, 3 inches; from the center of the middle pair to the center of the front pair, was 6 feet, 9 inches; making the entire distance between the extreme axles 12 feet. There was perhaps ½ inch end play on the axle of the back pair of wheels, none to the middle, or crank axle, and about ¼ inch in the front axle. The engine had inside cylinders, inclined so as to allow the cross-heads to clear the forward axle. There was an equalizing bar between the middle and hind pairs of wheels, and an independent spring over the forward pair.

The performance of this engine in the transportation of freight is mentioned as extremely good, and it is stated that the engine travels through a curve with all the facility of an engine of the usual pattern.

One of Hinkley's ten wheelers on the Northern road was altered by taking out the truck frame and putting in another pair of drivers. This could be done only by setting the new drivers very far forward, and by springing up the smoke-box end of the engine, as the cylinders in this pattern, though somewhat inclined, were not intended to admit another pair of driving wheels. The distance between the extreme axles of this engine is 15 ft. 6 in.; the two middle pairs of wheels have no flanges, and no end play was allowed in any of the boxes. The engine is said to draw a much greater load than when running with the truck frame, and is also said to ride as freely around a curve as before the alteration was made.

We have never believed the use of extra large wheels on our narrow gauge roads would afford proper grounds for their general introduction. The high point at which the power of the steam must be applied to work a seven or eight feet wheel, gives the engine greater leverage in its action on the rails, and consequently involves an increased expenditure for repairs, both on the road and on the machine. The use of large wheels presents a choice of two bad arrangements: the boiler, to get an inside connection, must set very high, so as to clear the cranks; while the only means of reducing the height of the boiler is to carry the cylinders outside, and to subject the whole engine to an injurious and sometimes dangerous oscillating motion, owing to the comparatively wide distance between the points at which the power is applied. Whichever plan may be adopted is found to possess its disadvantages. True, a pair of large drivers may be placed *behind* the fire-box, but *one* pair of wheels, and at that point also, does not give the engine sufficient adhesion to the rails.

On the whole, we do not believe the proposed advantages supposed to result from the use of a 3-feet stroke will ever compensate for the injurious effects of outside cylinders, with large wheels. The present speed of railroad travelling is as great as can be economically maintained, and any attempt to increase it increases in a higher ratio the expense of repairs and renewals. In support of our opinion we can confidently assert that no instance can be adduced of a narrow gauge engine in this country, having a wheel larger than six feet, where it has been thoroughly tested and its use approved of. The high speeds attained by 5½-feet wheels, with the express trains on the Worcester road, prove that a very rapid rate of travelling may be reached with an ordinary sized wheel.

Although we regard the only sure means of running quick to be found in perfecting and smoothing our roads, reducing the grades, easing the curves, and laying the road with more care for smoothness and stability, still we do not deny that a large wheel would be better for light express trains, running chiefly to transmit important despatches ; we do not, however, think the use of such engines would be advisable in running our regular and heavy trains.

There are many roads where trains of two or three cars are run by twenty two-ton engines. The injury sustained by the permanent way, from the continued passage of such unnecessarily heavy machines, has drawn a considerable degree of attention to the subject by practical, railroad men, both in this country and in Europe. On the Eastern Counties line, in England, a steam carriage, having engine, tank, and car, on one frame, the engine having 8 in. cyl., 12 in. stroke, 5 ft. wheel, and 255 feet heating surface, and the car capable of seating 84 passengers, was placed upon a branch road, and was found to require but 11½ lbs. of coke per mile, against 31½ lbs., the average amount consumed by the heavy engines before used. The whole carriage, in working trim, weighed 15 tons, 7 cwt., and with an additional car, making accommodation in all for 150 passengers, ran at an average rate of 37 miles per hour. The use of this mode of traffic, where admissible, is attended with a great diminution in the working expenses, and in the repairs of the line where it is employed.

To carry 120 passengers on the present system, the weight of engine, 22 tons, tender, wood and water, 15 tons, baggage car, 8 tons, and 2 passenger cars, 20 tons, must be included. This gives upwards of 1,200 lbs. dead weight to each passenger carried, or a train of 75 tons, at an average speed of 30 miles per hour.

SECTION IX.

Tables and Calculations relative to the Locomotive.

It is a very useful and interesting mental exercise to calculate the power, capacity, and other particulars of a locomotive. By an acquaintance with the expressed values of engines, deduced from natural principles, or being perhaps the results of experimental research, our minds become habituated to a better conception of their properties. At the same time, we require to have the means of knowing the capabilities of any machine in order to direct or suggest any improvements in its arrangement; and likewise to know that we are in possession of all the capabilities in the engine, which science can point out.

We therefore commence this section with a table which we have computed for the lengths of stroke and diameters of wheels of our American engines, and which is intended to express the speed of the piston compared with that of the circumference of the driving wheel, the speed of the latter being taken as 1. The use of this table we shall immediately proceed to show.

DIAM. OF DRIVERS.

Stroke of Piston.	42 in.	43 in.	46 in.	48 in.	54 in.	60 in.	66 in.	72 in.	78 in.	84 in.
16in.	.2425	.2369	.2214	.2122	.1886	.1697	.1543	.1415	.1306	.1213
18	.2728	.2665	.2491	.2387	.2122	.1910	.1736	.1591	.1469	.1364
20	.3031	.2961	.2768	.2652	.2358	.2122	.1929	.1768	.1632	.1516
22	.3335	.3257	.3045	.2918	.2594	.2334	.2122	.1945	.1795	.1668
24	.3639	.3554	.3321	.3183	.2829	.2546	.2315	.2122	.1959	.1819

Now to calculate the tractive force of a locomotive: multiply the sum of the areas of the two pistons by the effective pressure per square inch, the effective pressure being understood as the pressure in the boiler minus the pressure of steam barely sufficient to keep the engine and tender by themselves just in motion;—having the product so obtained, multiply it still further by the decimal coefficient corresponding to its length of stroke and diameter of wheel, as found in the preceding table; this last product expresses the tractive force of the engine, in pounds.

To illustrate the meaning of *traction*, we will suppose a deep pit to be sunk in the middle of a level track; let a weight in the bottom of the pit have a rope attached to it, the rope passing over a pulley, at the mouth of the pit, and being secured at its other end to the draw iron of a locomotive. The weight which the engine could raise in this manner, entirely through the adhesion of its drivers, is equal to the tractive force of the engine.

Example. What is the tractive power of a locomotive having 17-inch cylinders, 22-inch stroke, 43-inch wheels, and effective pressure 80 lbs. per square inch?

The area of a 17-inch piston is 226.98 sq. inches.
" two cylinders, therefore, 453.96 " "

And 453.96
80
———
36316.80
.3257 the coefficient of the given wheel and stroke.
———
11828.38 lbs., the product, which is the traction of the engine. The traction varies, however, according to the weight of the engine, for which this calculation does not provide.

The resistance offered by the *friction* of one ton on

a level railroad is the same as that of drawing up through the pit a weight of 10 pounds.* That is, 10 lbs. weight attached to a load of one ton, and passing over a pulley so as to act with its full weight on the load, would keep it in motion. Hence, to find how many tons the above engine would draw on a level, divide the traction already found by 10, the amount of traction necessary to overcome the friction of one ton on a level, and the quotient is the desired answer.

Thus: 10)11828(1182$\frac{4}{5}$ tons drawn by the 17-inch cylinder engine on a level.

Another rule for obtaining the traction of an engine, and deduced from the above, is to multiply the effective pressure per square inch by the square of the diameter of the cylinder, that product by the length of stroke, and divide the whole by the diameter of the wheel in inches. Thus, the above example would become, —

289 square of 17-inch cylinder.
80 lbs. pressure of steam.

23120
22 length of stroke.

43)508640(11828 lbs., as before.

The application of this rule, it will be seen, does not require the use of the table of decimal coefficients.

In going up a grade there is a certain tendency to roll down the hill, occasioned by the force of gravity. A portion of the tractive power of the engine is to be expended in overcoming this tendency of *gravity*, as well as the *friction* of the load.

To obtain the gravity, in pounds, of one ton on any grade: multiply 2240, the number of pounds in a ton,

* On a smooth road, with cars in good condition, the friction is 8, and sometimes as low as 7 pounds per ton.

by the height of the grade, and divide the product by the length of the grade. To obtain the gravity of one ton on a 47-feet grade, (the grade of Ward Hill, in Bradford, Mass.,) we multiply 2240 by 47, the height of the grade, and divide the product by 5280, the number of feet in one mile, or the length of the grade; the quotient is 19.9 lbs., which is the *gravity* of one ton on a grade of that pitch. To this must be added the *friction* of one ton, already given as 10 lbs., and the whole tractive power of the engine is to be divided by their amount, thus:

29.9)11832(395.7 tons, answer.

A simpler rule deduced from the above is to multiply the height of the grade per mile in feet, by the decimal .4242, which gives precisely the same answer; thus, 47 x .4242=19.9 + lbs.

N. B.—The weight of the engine and tender is *not* included in the above answers.

The friction of the engine and tender absorbs from 4 to 6 lbs. per square inch on the piston, and if the engine is not in good order, it will take more.

To find the quantity of water evaporated by an engine in going a certain distance, we can multiply the area of the piston by the length of stroke, or by that part of the stroke into which dense steam is admitted, where a cut-off is used; this gives the capacity of one cylinder, which, multiplied by four, gives the amount of steam used at one revolution. Then divide the distance of your journey by the circumference of the wheel, and make a discretionary allowance for slipping; this gives the number of revolutions made by the drivers in going the given distance, which, multiplied by the amount of steam used at one revolution, gives the entire quantity of steam used in going the entire distance. The question now arises, what part of this steam is water, or rather, what amount of water was required to generate this amount or volume of steam at the given pressure? We can ascertain this by reference to the table on page 12. Suppose the given pressure of steam was 110 lbs. per square inch; opposite this pressure in the table is 241, the number of cubic inches of steam generated under a pressure of 110 lbs. per inch from one cubic inch of water. Divide, therefore, the whole amount of steam of 110 lbs. used in the journey, by 241, and you have the amount of water evaporated to generate that steam.

Ex. How many gallons of water would an engine evaporate in running the distance from Boston to Lowell, 26 miles, the engine being of the following dimensions: 15-inch cylinder, 18-inch stroke, 5-feet wheel, pressure 100 lbs. per inch, and cutting off at half stroke?

176.71 area of 15-inch piston in square inches.
9 = inches of stroke into which dense steam is admitted.

1590.39 amount of steam used by one cyl. at one stk.
4

6361.56 amount of steam used at one revolution.

Now get the distance in 26 miles by multiplying by 5280, the number of feet in a mile, thus:

5280
26

15.708)137280(8739 revolutions in going 26 miles, the divisor, 15.708, being the circumference of the driver in feet and decimals.

The number of revolutions, 8739, being multiplied by the quantity of steam used at one revolution, 6361.5 cubic inches, the product is 55593148 cubic inches of steam used in going 26 miles. Now the pressure is 100 lbs.; and by the table on page 12, one cubic inch of water makes 260 cubic inches of steam of that pressure. Now the whole quantity of steam used, divided by 260, gives the quantity of water evaporated to generate that steam, which is, we find by dividing, 213819 cubic inches; and this amount, divided by 231, the number of cubic inches in a wine gallon, gives 925.6 gallons used, which corresponds very nearly with the actual quantity used by an engine of the given dimensions, and running on the Lowell road. It will be seen we have made no allowances for slipping, nor for any loss of steam by blowing off.

We sometimes wish to know the amount of advantage gained by using steam expansively; that is, the advantage gained by cutting off steam at any fraction of the stroke. Suppose the induction port to a cylinder to remain open during one stroke of the piston, thereby admitting steam enough to fill the entire capacity of the cylinder, and of the same pressure as within the boiler. We will then suppose the amount of work done or load raised by that engine to be represented by the number 3. Take then the same cylinder, place the piston at the end of the stroke, and admit steam by the valve until the piston has gone through one-third the distance of the stroke. Now the load raised by the engine is either the same load as when full steam was used, but to only one-third the distance, or one-third of the former load to the same distance. In either case the work done is represented by one-third the number used to represent the former load, and that number being 3, the work done when the piston has gone through one-third of its stroke is 1. But when the piston is at that point of its stroke, one-third of the length of the cylinder is filled with steam of the same pressure as in the boiler; this steam therefore acts upon the piston, at first with its full pressure, but as the piston moves along, thereby increasing the capacity of that end of the cylinder, the steam expands and presses with a diminished force, until the piston has arrived at the extreme of its stroke; when the steam which was admitted until the piston was at one-third stroke, has now become expanded into three times its original volume, and thereby has only one-third of its original pressure remaining. But it has pressed upon the piston with a constantly diminishing force during the last two-thirds of the stroke, and has thereby contributed to the useful effect of the engine. The steam originally admitted, after performing an amount of work represented by the number 1, has performed during the last two-thirds of the stroke a still further amount of work, which in reality should be represented by a number a trifle over 1, making the entire useful effect derived from one-third of a cylinder full of steam, a trifle more than two-thirds of what it was when a full cylinder of steam was used. It is evident that none of this additional useful effect, derived from the expansive property of steam, could have been obtained had steam of full pressure been constantly admitted upon the piston throughout its whole stroke. Were there sufficient steam in a boiler to fill a given cylinder 12 times full, the pressure in the cylinder being the same as in the boiler, and the work performed by using this steam through the whole stroke of the piston to be represented by 12, it follows that by filling only one-third of the length of the cylinder at each stroke, there would be sufficient steam for 36 strokes, the effect of each being represented by $\frac{2}{3}$, and of the whole, 24 or twice the effect obtained by using the steam at full stroke. And thus it appears that although you can never obtain the full effect of the engine except with full steam, still, more work can be done by expansion, when compared with the amount of steam used. Hence there is a very great economy in employing full steam through but a portion of the stroke, letting the stroke be completed by the expansion of the steam already in the cylinder.

Again, this principle of expanding the steam in the cylinder, while it reduces the quantity of steam used, has no effect on the production of steam in the boiler, other than what results from throwing a surplus pressure, as it accumulates, upon the water level. By tracing the practical applications of this advantage, we find a given boiler may supply a larger cylinder, or a given cylinder may be supplied by a smaller boiler, and do more work than with the original proportions before expansion. With expansion, therefore, the same work may be performed with a reduction in the weight of the engine, which is a very important advantage. The less the resistance of the load, the greater may be the extent to which expansion is carried in the cylinder, and for this reason expedients are sometimes resorted to for adapting the expansion to the resistance of the train.

Having thus explained the philosophy which dictates the use of expansion or cut-off valves, we will give a table by which the effect of the engine may be estimated for any amount of expansion. This table is called a table of hyperbolic logarithms, and as an explanation of the manner in which the table is prepared would encroach upon our limits, and at the same time be foreign to the character of our work, we will confine ourselves to the manner of employing this table, for the purpose of calculating the effect due to the expansion of steam. We will first present the table.

TABLE OF HYPERBOLIC LOGARITHMS.

No.	Hyp. Log.	No.	Hyp. Log.	No.	Hyp. Log.	No.	Hyp. Log.
1.05	.049	2.05	.718	3.05	1.115	4.05	1.399
1.1	.095	2.1	.742	3.1	1.131	4.1	1.411
1.15	.140	2.15	.765	3.15	1.147	4.15	1.423
1.2	.182	2.2	.788	3.2	1.163	4.2	1.435
1.25	.223	2.25	.811	3.25	1.179	4.25	1.447
1.3	.262	2.3	.833	3.3	1.194	4.3	1.459
1.35	.300	2.35	.854	3.35	1.209	4.35	1.470
1.4	.336	2.4	.875	3.4	1.224	4.4	1.482
1.45	.372	2.45	.896	3.45	1.238	4.45	1.493
1.5	.405	2.5	.916	3.5	1.253	4.5	1.504
1.55	.438	2.55	.936	3.55	1.267	4.55	1.515
1.6	.470	2.6	.956	3.6	1.281	4.6	1.526
1.65	.500	2.65	.975	3.65	1.295	4.65	1.537
1.7	.531	2.7	.993	3.7	1.308	4.7	1.548
1.75	.560	2.75	1.012	3.75	1.322	4.75	1.558
1.8	.588	2.8	1.030	3.8	1.335	4.8	1.569
1.85	.615	2.85	1.047	3.85	1.348	4.85	1.579
1.9	.642	2.9	1.065	3.9	1.361	4.9	1.589
1.95	.668	2.95	1.082	3.95	1.374	4.95	1.599
2	.693	3	1.099	4	1.386	5	1.609

To use this table in estimating the gain by expansive force: — Divide the whole length of the stroke by the distance through which the piston travels before the closing of the cut-off valve; find in the table the hyperbolic logarithm of the quotient, add 1 to it, and the amount is the ratio of uniform and expansive force.

Example. Let the stroke of a locomotive be 18 inches, and the steam cut off at 12 inches; what is the ratio of the gain? 18 divided by 12 gives for the quotient $1\frac{1}{2}$. The hyperbolic logarithm corresponding to this number in the table is .405, (which we must remember is decimal;) and adding unity to it, it becomes 1.405, the effect by cutting off at $\frac{2}{3}$ stroke as compared with 1.5 the effect when using full steam, or .937 of the effect of full steam by using but $\frac{2}{3}$ steam.

In getting the heating surface and capacity of a boiler, we require every extent of surface in the parts which determine the shape and size of the boiler, in order to arrive at a correct result. To get the contents of the water room in a boiler, we must first find the diameter of the boiler in inches, and find by calculation, its corresponding sectional area. To obtain the area of water section, deduct the sectional area of all the tubes from one-half the sectional area of the boiler; then find the average between the width of the center of the boiler, that is, its diameter, and the width of the water level, and multiply this average by the depth of water above the center of the boiler. This, added to the water section in the lower half of the boiler, gives the entire water section. Now, multiply this by the length of the cylindrical part of the boiler; multiply the width, depth and thickness of the water spaces together; make the proper deduction in the contents of the back water space for the door, and in the front water space for the tubes, which pass through it; multiply the area of the crown sheet by the depth of water on its surface, and make the proper deduction for the stay bars; and the entire contents in cubic inches, divided by 1728 for cubic feet, or by 231 for wine gallons, will give a pretty accurate result for the capacity of the boiler.

The steam room of the boiler is calculated very much in the same way. The steam section in the cylindrical part of the boiler is obtained by deducting the water section and tube section from the boiler's sectional area, this being multiplied by the length of the cylindrical part of the boiler, as for the water content. As the circle of the outside fire-box is generally a little larger than that of the boiler, a separate calculation should be made for this part. The content of the dome must also be found, and a deduction made for the steam pipe. In getting the extent of heating surface on the tubes, we must calculate it from the outer circumference of the tubes; for, although the fire is only in contact with their inner circumferences, the whole thickness of the tube becomes heated, so that the outer circumference has the same temperature to heat the water as the inner circumference receives from the fire. The English engineers reckon the tube surface of a locomotive as but one-third as effective as the fire-box surface, so that an engine with 54 square feet of fire-box surface, and 660 square feet of tube surface, would be reckoned as having only 54 plus 220, or 274 square feet of heating surface.

In getting the fire-box surface we should reckon every square inch of heated surface in contact with the water, which would of course be the four sides and the crown sheet, deducting only the areas of the outsides of the tubes, and the space occupied by the door, and the bar riveted around it. The heating surface of the fire-box could not be considered as extending below the grate. We have already said that the practice is sometimes to reckon only the back, sides, and top of the fire-box as heating surface, but we should suppose that a man having woodland, pasturage and mowing land, might with as much propriety give the size of his mowing fields for the size of his farm.

The surface of the grate is of course simply the length and breadth multiplied together.

We have already given the manner of calculating the ratios of the safety valve levers, on page 63.

There can properly be no such expression as the horse power of a locomotive. The difference between a stationary and a locomotive engine, is such that while the former *raises* a load, or overcomes any directly opposing resistance, with an effect due to its capacity of cylinder, the load of the locomotive is *drawn*, and its resistance must be adapted to the simple *adhesion* of the engine, and which may be varied even as the rims of the wheels are of wrought or cast iron, as the rails are in good or bad order, as the grades of the track, the speed of the engine, and various unsettled circumstances which cannot well be resolved so as to give an expression of the power of the locomotive in the term, horses' power.

Stationary steam engines are applied to a vast variety of purposes, but locomotives are only required for one kind of work. A cotton manufacturer negotiating for a steam engine would not care to know how many feet of lumber were sawed, nor how many bushels of grain were ground by a certain sized engine, nor would a miller wish to know the power of an engine for spinning cotton or weaving cloth. The standard of a *horse power* serves as a standard of comparison, and its utility as a unit of reference is not impaired whether it represent the actual power of one horse, or three, so long as the standard is universal. But as the work of a locomotive is all of one character, it becomes an object to know the actual power of an engine in drawing freight or passengers, in preference to referring it to any doubtful standard, not expressing its capabilities. This we have illustrated at the commencement of this section, but for the assistance of such as may have occasion to estimate the horses' power of a stationary, or even a locomotive engine, we will give the usual rule. It is as follows: multiply the area of the piston, the pressure of steam per square inch, the number of revolutions per minute, and the length of stroke together, divide the product by 33,000, and take $\frac{7}{10}$ of the quotient for the effective horses' power of the engine.

It is a received law in mechanical science, that the effect of a machine is to be estimated from its weight or elemental power multiplied into the space through which the power acts. Our readers will detect that in the above rule we have directions to employ but *one-half* the speed of the piston to get the power of the engine. For instance, a 16-inch cylinder engine is usually rated as a 50-horse engine; but if in calculating its power we employ the actual speed of the piston in feet per minute, we shall find our engine to have 100 horses' power.

If a horse raise 150 lbs. through 220 feet in a minute, or, through the application of wheels and axles, levers, &c., he raise 33,000 lbs. one foot high in a minute, then what is usually termed a one-horse engine will raise 66,000 lbs. through the same distance and in the same time. We have always supposed that the reason for taking but one-half the speed of the piston in estimating the power of an engine, arose from the fact that the steam engine was employed on its first introduction in pumping water from mines, and for raising water for towns, where only one stroke of the engine was effectual. A horse may raise a constant load of 33,000 lbs. one foot per minute, but in pumping he could raise but half that sum, for one-half of his time would be expended in driving the piston of the pump downwards. Hence though our present allowance for a horse's power answers every purpose for a standard of reference to determine merely the comparative power of engines, still we shall contend that our usual manner of getting the power of an engine gives us but one-half the proper amount of its capabilities.

We will give an example illustrating the rule we have given for estimating the horses' power of a steam engine.

What is the horses' power of an engine, having a 14-inch cylinder, 42-inch stroke, the pressure of steam being 71 lbs. per square inch, and the fly-wheel making 37 revolutions per minute? N. B.—The speed of the piston to be obtained in the usual manner, by multiplying the number of revolutions into the length of stroke.

153.94 sq. in. area of a 14-inch piston.
71 lbs. per square inch.

10929.74 lbs. entire pressure on the piston.

Now we wish to ascertain the number of feet the piston travels per minute, or rather half the actual number:

37 number of rev. per min.
$3\frac{1}{2}$ length of stroke in feet.

129.5 speed of piston in feet per min.

10929.74 pressure on piston.
129.5 speed of piston.

33000)1415401 (42.9 horse power.

And $\frac{7}{10}$ of this quotient is 30 horses' power, the power of the engine.

To get the capacity of a tender tank, we must first obtain the extent of surface on the bottom of the tank, which, multiplied by its height or depth, and reduced to gallons, gives its capacity. To illustrate this calculation, we will give a diagram of Hinkley's tank for a six-wheeled tender.

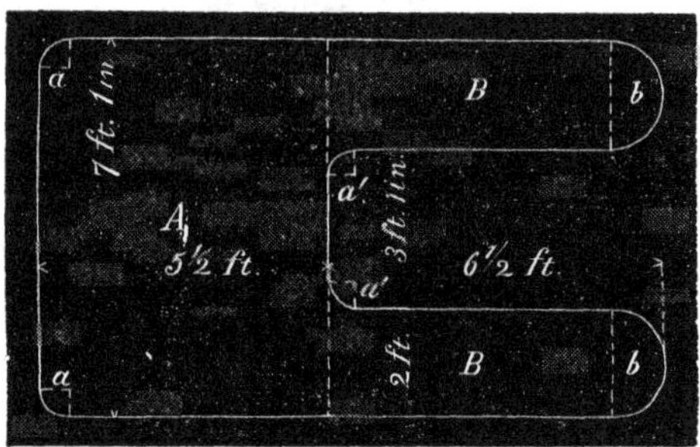

Radius of corners a, a, and a', a', 6 inches.
Depth of tank 35 inches.

The part A may be considered as an exact parallelogram, since the surface cut off by the corners a, a, is again made up by those at a', a'. The sum of the two semicircular terminations b, b, of the wings B, B, has of course the area of one entire circle two feet in diameter; and these semicircles reduce the length of the straight part of the wings B, B, one foot. Hence the area of the surface of the tank is as follows:

85 x 66	5610	area of part A.
66 x 24 x 2	3168	" " wings B, B.
	452	" " terminations *b*, *b*.
	9230	sq. in. surface of tank.
	35	depth of tank.
	323050	cub. inches in tank.

This last product, expressing the contents of the tank in cubic inches, may be divided by 231, and we shall have the capacity of the tank in gallons. This we find to be 1398½ gallons.

The young machinist will readily perceive there is no difficulty in making any of these calculations, as they involve only the simplest rules of arithmetic, while their solution forms a very useful and interesting mental exercise. It is an excellent idea for any one wishing to get thoroughly acquainted with the steam engine, to measure and preserve the proportions of every engine that may come in his way; these dimensions sooner or later assume a high value to the possessor, inasmuch as he finds them convenient for reference in comparison, estimation, or in designing new work. They also serve to bring him in closer acquaintance with the principles of the mechanical science involved in the theory and the practical construction of the steam engine.

To get the area of a circle. Square its diameter, that is to say, multiply the diameter into itself, and multiply this product by the decimal number .7854; the last product will be the area of the circle.

Example 1. What is the area of a 17-inch piston?

```
    17
    17
 ------
   289
 .7854
 ------
226.98 square inches area, answer.
```

Example 2. What is the sectional area of a steam pipe 4½ inches inside diameter?

```
    4.5
    4.5
  ------
  20.25
  .7854
  ------
15.904 square inches area, answer.
```

N. B.—In multiplying with decimal numbers, we must recollect to point off as many places from the right hand of the product for decimals, as there are places of decimals in the multiplier and multiplicand taken together.

To get the circumference of a circle, multiply the diameter by 3.1416, the product is the circumference.

Another method is to multiply the diameter by 355, and to divide the product by 113. To those accustomed to proportion, this rule might be presented thus:

113 : 355 : : diameter : circumference.

These two numbers may be readily carried in the mind from a slight peculiarity in the order of their arrangement. By setting the two numbers down in the following manner, it will be seen there are two ones, two threes, and two fives, thus: 113355.

Examples. What is the circumference of a copper tube 2 inches in diameter?

$$\begin{array}{r} 3.1416 \\ 2 \\ \hline 6.2832 \end{array}$$ inches, answer.

What is the circumference of a driving wheel $66\frac{1}{2}$ inches in diameter?

$$\begin{array}{r} 66.5 \\ 355 \\ \hline \end{array}$$

113)23607.5(208.9 in., answer.

N. B.—In dividing with decimal numbers, we must point off as many places for decimals in the quotient, as, taken with those in the divisor, if any, will equal the nnmber of decimal places in the dividend. Division is the reverse of multiplication, and the divisor and quotient are factors, of which the dividend is the product.

What is the circumference of a 5-feet driving wheel? Five feet reduced to inches, becomes 60 inches.

355
60

113)21300(188.496 inches, answer.

TABLE OF THE AREAS OF PISTONS.

Diam.	Area.	Diam.	Area.
10 in.	78.540	14½ in.	165.130
10½	86.590	*14¾	170.873
11	95.033	15	176.715
11½	103.869	15½	188.692
12	113.097	16	201.062
12½	122.718	16½	213.825
13	132.732	17	226.980
13½	143.139	17½	240.528
14	153.938	18	254.469

TABLE OF THE CIRCUMFERENCES OF DRIVERS.

Diam.	Circumference.	Diam.	Circumference.
42 in.	131.94 in.	60 in.	188.50 in.
43 "	135.08 "	66 "	207.34 "
46 "	144.51 "	72 "	226.19 "
48 "	150.80 "	78 "	245.04 "
54 "	169.64 "	84 "	263.89 "

* Size of Grigg's cylinders on the Providence Road.

SECTION X.

Miscellaneous Notes and Observations.

THE principal locomotive concerns in this country at the present time, are the following:

Portland Locomotive Works, Portland, Maine,
Horace Felton, Superintendent.
Amoskeag Manufacturing Co., Manchester, N. H.,
Oliver W. Bayley, Superintendent.
Essex Company at Lawrence, Mass.,
Caleb M. Marvell, Superintendent.
Lowell Machine Shop at Lowell, Mass.,
William A. Burke, Superintendent.
Boston Locomotive Works, Boston, Hinkley, Drury, and others, Proprietors,
D. T. Child, Treasurer.
Union Works, South Boston,
Seth Wilmarth, Proprietor.
Globe Works, South Boston,
John Souther, Proprietor.
Taunton Locomotive Manufacturing Company, Taunton, Mass., W. W. Fairbanks, Agent.
Matteawan Machine Works, Fishkill Landing, New York, W. B. Leonard, Agent.
Norris Locomotive Works, Schenectady, N. Y.,
Edward S. Norris, Proprietor.
Rogers, Ketchum, and Grosvenor, Paterson, N. J.
Swinburn and Smith, Paterson, N. J.
Ross Winans, Baltimore, Md.
Baldwin and Whitney, Philadelphia, Pa.
Norris, Brothers, Philadelphia, Pa.

Denmead at Baltimore, a shop at Richmond, Va.,

and an establishment at Cleveland, Ohio, also advertise to build locomotives.

In Boston, the Maine, the Providence, and the Worcester Railroads have built many engines for themselves.

The Springfield Car and Engine Co., and the Ballardvale Machine Shop at Andover, Mass., have been nearly closed, and the manufacture of locomotives at those places has been entirely suspended.

Jabez Coney, of South Boston, built at his shop, in 1847, two locomotives for the Old Colony road.

The price of a first class 21-ton passenger engine, varies according to the style from 6800 to 8000 dollars. Freight engines, from being built from heavier patterns, generally cost more.

Below we give estimates of the weights of some of the *principal* parts about a locomotive, and about the average prices usually charged for such items.

42-inch boiler, 7500 lbs., a 14c. -	$1050.00
135, 1¾-inch copper flues, 10½ feet long, 2500 lbs., a 30c. - - - -	750.00
Turning and driving thimbles, setting do. &c.	30.00
Solid engine frame, 2500 lbs. a 6c. -	150.00
Jaws of wrought iron, 1000 lbs. a 10c. -	100.00
Finishing frame, - - - - -	150.00
4 Driving wheels, for 5½ ft. di. 6000 lbs. a 3c.	180.00
1 Crank axle, 6½ in. finish, 1500 lbs. a 18c.	270.00
1 Straight axle, 650 lbs. a 10c. - -	65.00
2 Truck axles, 3½ in. journals, 480 lbs. a 6c.	28.80
4 Truck wheels, 30 in. diameter, - -	70.00
4 Lowmoor tires, 5½ ft. 2850 lbs. a 13c. -	370.50
Finishing wheels, cranks, and axles, -	200.00
2 Cylinder castings, 15 inches in diameter, 1600 lbs. a 3c. - - - -	48.00
Boring cylinders, - - - - - -	50.00
2 Rough connecting rods, 360 lbs. a 8c, -	28.80

The prices given are perhaps a fair average, and the whole table may serve to show about the usual weight of the heavier and more important parts of a locomotive.

In regard to explosions, we do not believe any well made boiler ever gave way to do any serious damage, except through a want of water in it. If the water is suffered to get below the upper row of tubes, the fire generally burns them out, the water rushes into the fire-box and extinguishes the fire, thus preventing all danger; but enginemen have sometimes found their water entirely run down, and the flues entirely spoilt by the fire, but not burnt out. We recollect, and perhaps others who may read this will recollect also, of an instance on the Lowell and Lawrence road where an officer of the road undertook the management of an engine, and succeeded in boiling every drop of water away, burning the wooden lagging off the boiler, and burning the tubes so as to make it necessary to replace every one of them, though they were not burnt through. When the water is boiled entirely away, and the internal shell of the boiler becomes heated red hot, the admission of cold water generally produces an explosion. Some attribute this to the immediate decomposition of the nitrogen, one of the principal gases which enter into the composition of water, and leaving the hydrogen to explode by the intense heat. But the presence of oxygen is necessary for the explosion of hydrogen gas, and a very distinguished chemist has averred that there can be no oxygen in a boiler filled with steam. A recent theory is that of the spheroidal state of water when thrown upon a red hot plate. The water, it is stated, when thrown upon a plate heated to a very high rate of temperature, assumes the spheroidal state, rolling over the plate in smooth globules, like a mass of melted lead; while in this state no steam can be produced from the water; but when the temperature of the plate falls to a certain extent, the water becomes almost instantaneously converted into steam of intense and overwhelming elasticity, and the consequence is, the boiler gives way in the weakest part.

We would not wish to revive in this place the question of the explosion on the Providence road, about which there was so much diversity of opinion; but we must say, that in *that* instance, the report of the commission, notwithstanding its high authority, hardly succeeded in satisfying the minds of a large portion of the public.

A recent act of the Massachusetts Legislature requires that the boiler of every stationary, locomotive or marine engine, running within the State, shall have a fusible plug in the crown sheet of the furnace. To answer this requirement, a lead plug ½ inch in diam. is tapped into the crown sheet of a locomotive furnace, so that when the top of the fire-box becomes uncovered with water, this plug may melt, and by letting the steam escape into the fire-box, give notice of the danger.

At the introduction of railroads, engines were built with cylinders no larger than 8 inches in diameter. In 1840, we think there were no engines with cylinders larger than 12 inches. In 1844, we had 13½-inch cylinders, by '47, 15 inches; and now Perkins, on the Baltimore and Ohio Road, is building an engine with a 20-inch cylinder. The gauge of our roads remains the same now as it was a dozen or fifteen years ago,—four feet eight and one-half inches inside the rails. In those days two trains per day, drawn by the light engines, were all which the business of a road would warrant. Now we have twenty to thirty trains drawn over our principal roads daily, by engines averaging from twenty to twenty-five tons in weight. These facts are sufficient to show a vast increase of business wherever railroads are extended. This constantly growing traffic must, at no distant period, demand the adoption of a wider gauge for our tracks. Railroad men prefer engines with inside cylinders to those having the cylinders outside. Every engine requires apparatus for reversing and for working expansively, and no better means, we think, have yet been found to effect these objects than the use of six eccentrics. Here the insufficiency of the width of the track becomes evident; it is only by economizing every inch of room that sufficient space can be found to arrange the work of an inside cylinder engine. It would be a matter of very great convenience were the track wider than at present, and we believe that the experience of a dozen years at most, will determine it to be a matter of absolute necessity. The gauge of the Atlantic and St. Lawrence, and the Androscoggin and Kennebec roads, in Maine, is five feet six inches inside the rails, and that of the New York and Erie railroad is six feet. Wherever a break of gauge is made, it would seem of importance that the addition in width should be uniform on all roads, as a difference in tracks disturbs the traffic, inasmuch as no means exist of forwarding goods by such roads, except by changing cars.

Every railroad doing any considerable amount of business should have sufficient and capacious repair shops of its own. The increased facility and convenience with which they can do their own repairs, and the saving in the profits which outside shops charge them, make it a matter of economy to repair their own work. For a railroad having fifteen to twenty locomotives, a shop 120 by 60 feet, and one story high, if properly laid out, makes a very convenient repair shop. For such a shop there would probably be required for tools, &c.,

One stationary steam engine (25 horse,) say	$1500
" Locomotive boiler with wro't iron flues, -	1800
" Large engine lathe to swing six feet, -	1500
" 14 feet planing machine, - - -	800
" 12 " engine lathe with screw feed, -	350
" 12 " do. do. without do. -	300
" 10 " do. do. do. do. -	250
" Hand lathe for iron, - - -	175
" do. do. " wood, - - -	125
" Bolt cutting machine, - - -	250
" Wall drill, - - - - - -	125
" Suspended drill for tires, - - -	125
" Machine for drawing on wheels, - -	50
" Blower for blacksmith's shop, - -	50
" Forge hammer, - - - - -	400
Total, - -	$7800

We merely give the above estimate to show with how few tools and at how little expense the repairing department of a railroad may be conducted. In arranging such a shop, however, the fancy or belief of many would lead them to have many additional tools, such as one 16-feet engine lathe, a compound planer, (the expense of these two being about $1000) ; and for an increased business, some would think a spliner ($500,) and some other tools necessary. We know, however, of some roads having twenty locomotives, and doing all their repairs with a list of tools such as is comprised in our original estimate.

We give below the particulars of the weight and performance of some of the heaviest engines on the Fitchburg road, from the Directors' Report for 1849. The whole number of engines on the road on the 31st of December, 1849, was twenty-five.

N. B.—The following engines were built by Hinkley, with the exception of the "Boston," which was built by Lyman and Souther, of South Boston.

Athol,	15 in.	cyl.	20 in.	stroke,	four $4\frac{1}{2}$	ft.	drivers,	&	truck	outside cl.
Concord,	15 "	"	20 "	"	" $4\frac{1}{2}$	"	"	"	"	" "
Shirley,	14 "	"	18 "	"	" 5	"	"	"	"	inside "
Lincoln,	16 "	"	20 "	"	" $4\frac{1}{2}$	"	"	"	"	" "
Camb'dge,	15 "	"	18 "	"	" 5	"	"	"	"	" "
Littleton,	15 "	"	18 "	"	" 5	"	"	"	"	" "
Boston,	16 "	"	20 "	"	" $5\frac{1}{2}$	"	"	"	"	" "
Fitchburg,	16 "	"	20 "	"	" 5	"	"	"	"	" "
Ontario,	16 "	"	20 "	"	six 46 in.		"	"	"	" "

Names.	Weight of Engine in running order.	Weight on Drivers.	Weight of Tender with wood and water.	Capacity of Tender.		Wheels on Tender.	Miles run in 1849.
	lbs.	lbs.	lbs.	Galls. wat'r.	Cords wood.		
Athol,	40,000	30,000	27,000	1,400	1	six.	10,419
Concord,	40,000	30,000	27,000	1,400	1	"	19,348
Shirley,	34,000	24,000	23,700	1,200	1	"	23,222
Lincoln,	46,600	30,900	29,000	1,600	$1\frac{1}{2}$	eight.	19,050
Cambridge,	40,000	28,000	27,752	1,400	1	six.	25,182
Littleton,	40,000	28,000	27,700	1,400	1	"	25,474
Boston,	46,000	30,000	30,000	1,500	$1\frac{1}{2}$	eight.	29,000
Fitchburg,	46,600	30,900	29,000	1,600	$1\frac{1}{3}$	"	12,792
Ontario,	47,000	36,000	28,058	1,600	$1\frac{1}{3}$	"	9,515

The "Champlain," an engine of the same dimensions as the "Ontario," ran 24,628 miles in the same time.

In regard to the strength of boiler iron and the effects of high temperatures upon it, it was ascertained from experiments made by a committee of the Franklin Institute, that at a temperature of 32°, the freezing point, the cohesive strength of boiler iron was $\frac{1}{7}$ below its maximum, and that its strength increased as an additional temperature was applied, until it had reached 570 degrees Fahrenheit, when the iron was found to have attained its maximum strength. Above this point the strength of the iron was diminished; at

720° it had the same cohesive strength as at 32°, or $\frac{1}{7}$ below its maximum; at 1050° one-half its greatest strength; at 1240°, one-third; and at 1317°, nearly one-seventh. Copper follows a different law, as every addition of temperature above the freezing point appears to weaken it. At 529°, it has but three-fourths its greatest strength; at 812°, but one-half; while a temperature of 1300° entirely destroys its cohesive force.

The adhesion of the wheels of an engine is about one-fifth the weight when the rails are clean, and either perfectly wet or perfectly dry, but only from one-tenth to one-twelfth the weight when the rails are damp or greasy. Thus, for a rough calculation, a 25-ton engine will have 5 tons adhesion, and as the resistance of a train on a level is about $\frac{1}{200}$, such an engine should draw, including its own weight and that of its tender, 1,000 tons on a level. This would be its maximum load at a slow speed.

We recollect the published report of the performance of one of Baldwin's six-driver engines, the "Ontario," in 1845, on the Philadelphia and Reading road. The train consisted of 150 cars fully loaded with coal, the weight of the coal being 759 tons, and of the coal and cars 1180 tons. The engine, it was stated, moved along alone with this extraordinary train at a rapid rate. A four-wheel engine, having its entire weight on the drivers, drew from Lowell to Boston, in July, 1849, a train of one hundred and twenty-nine cars, mostly loaded. This engine had 13½ inch cylinders.

☞ Having completed the original design of our little work, we would devote a spare page to some particulars of the present state of the railway system, which must prove interesting to all.

According to the Railroad Journal, there were at the commencement of 1849, 18656 miles of finished railroad in the world, costing £368,567,000, or about 1800 millions of dollars; also 7829 miles of unfinished road, which at the estimate of £146,750,000, would give in all, 26485 miles of railroad, costing 2400 millions of dollars, all of which has been invested since 1830!

In July, 1850, there were 7742 miles of Railroad in the United States, 2423 miles of which are in New England. Whole amount expended on roads in operation since 1834, $300,000,000.

At the end of 1848 there were in Great Britain and Ireland 5127 miles opened, 2111 miles in progress, and 4795 miles authorized, but not commenced. On 4253 miles opened, in United Kingdom, on May 1, 1848, there were 52,688 operatives. On 7388 miles of unopened road, there were 188,177 operatives. The total amount of money and securities paid into Railroad treasuries on these lines to the commencement of 1849, was one thousand millions of dollars, while the companies retained power to raise by existing shares, new shares, and loans, the further sum of £143,717,773.

In 1850, there were 24 roads in France, of 1722 miles, and including portions constructing, but not finished, 2996 miles. Average cost per mile, $128,240. Fare per mile: First class, $3.07; second class, $2.31; and third class, $1.77.

In 1849, there were 2294 miles of road opened, in Austria, Prussia, and the German States.

In Belgium, 347 miles, owned by government.

In Holland, about 110 miles.

In the north of Italy, there is a line, partly finished, from Venice to Turin and Alexandria. When the proposed tunnel beneath the Alps shall be completed, this road will form a main link in the great direct railroad line from London to the Adriatic.

There are short roads in nearly all the States of continental Europe, except in the States of the Church, where the Pope has opposed their introduction. And Russia, aided by American energy and skill, is opening a vast road between her two great capitals, Moscow and St. Petersburg.

A GLOSSARY

OF TERMS APPLIED TO THE MACHINERY, AND TO THE OPERATION OF THE LOCOMOTIVE ENGINE.

[N. B. Many of the names and terms here used, are explained at greater length in the body of the book.]

Adhesion. The measure of the friction between the tires of the driving wheels and the surfaces of the rails. The adhesion varies with the weight on the drivers and the state of the rails, but with a good rail is generally from one-fifth to one-seventh of the weight on the drivers. The load drawn is no measure of the adhesion, except the resistance of friction and gravity of the load be given.

Air Chamber. A tight vessel attached to the pump. The feed water, entering it at the bottom, is subjected to the pressure of air within it, which forces out the water in a steady stream. Recent engines have two air chambers to each pump, one on the suction, and one on the forcing side of the same. The capacity of air chamber should equal that of the barrel of the pump.

Angle of Friction. That pitch of grade at which a loaded car would just stand without descending, being kept at rest by the friction of its bearings. Allowing the friction to be 7 lbs. per ton, this grade would be 16½ feet per mile; for 10 lbs. friction per ton, 23½ feet per mile.

Ash Pan. A box or tray beneath the furnace, to catch the falling ashes and cinders.

Axle. The revolving shaft to which the wheels are secured.

Blast Pipes. Two pipes, contracted at their mouths to discharge the waste steam from the cylinders. Their action excites an artificial draft or blast in the furnace.

Blow-off Cock. A cock at the bottom of fire-box, through which to empty the boiler.

Boiler. The source of power; the vessel in which the steam is generated.

Bonnet. A wire cap or netting, surmounting the chimney to keep down the sparks and cinders.

Box. A bearing, enclosing the journal of a revolving shaft. When made in two parts, the lighter is called the cap. When made as a single piece, and supporting the end of an upright shaft, a step; and when turned outside and fitted into a frame, or stand, a bushing. To reduce friction, boxes are lined with soft metal.

Brake. A block or strap applied to the rim of a wheel, to check its motion, and bring it to a stop.

Bunters. Guards projecting from the ends of tenders and cars, and connected with springs, to prevent shocks from collisions.

Camb. A plate or pulley, turning on a shaft out of its center. When made round, and encircled by a strap, and employed to work the valves of a steam engine, and for similar purposes, is called an eccentric.

Case. A casting sliding in the jaw, and to hold the brass box of an axle. For drivers, the case is lined with Babbitt metal, and forms the bearing for the axle.

Check Valve. See *Valve.*

Counterbalance. A large block secured between two arms of each driving wheel, to balance the momentum of the moving machinery connected with the axle.

Connecting Rod. Rod to communicate the pressure on the piston to the crank.

Crank. In inside cylinder engines is forged in the axle, and for outside cylinders is supplied by a pin in the wheel. The crank converts the rectilineal motion of the piston to the rotary motion of the wheels.

Cross Head. A block moving in guides; having the end of

the piston rod secured within it at one side, and a pin to attach the connecting rod at the other.

Cut-off Valve. An additional valve, not indispensable, to shut off the admission of steam to the cylinder, when the piston has only completed a part of its stroke.

Cylinder. A cylindrical vessel, closed at its ends by covers. Steam is admitted alternately at each end, to press upon a block called the piston. The piston is made to fit, steam tight, to the inner circumference of the cylinder, and the action of the steam keeps it in motion, from one end of the cylinder to the other.

Damper. A door, to exclude the air from the furnace.

Dome. An elevated chamber on the top of the boiler, from which the steam is taken to the cylinders.

Draw Iron. A rigid bar, connecting the engine and tender, and secured to each by a pin.

Drivers, or Driving Wheels. Those wheels turned directly by the moving machinery of the engine, and which, by their adhesion to the rails, propel the engine along.

Eccentrics. See *Camb.*

Eduction Port. A passage on side of cylinder to lead away the waste steam from same, to the blast pipes.

Equalizing Lever. A bar suspended by its center, beneath the frame, and connected at each end to the springs of the drivers, to distribute any shock or jolt between both pairs of wheels.

Expansion Valve. See *Cut-off.*

Fire-box. The furnace of the boiler.

Foaming. An artificial excitement, or too great ebullition on the water level, observed when the boiler has become greasy, or otherwise foul. Generally productive of priming.

Footboard. A plate iron floor, behind the boiler, for the engineman and fireman to stand upon.

Frame. Made to attach to the boiler, cylinders, axles, and all cross shafts, and binds the whole fabric together.

Friction, of trains. The friction of the bearings of the carriages, and for every ton drawn, offers a direct resistance of from seven to ten pounds.

Frost Cocks. Cocks to admit steam to the feed pipes leading from the tender to the pump; used when the water becomes frozen.

Gauge Cocks. Cocks at different levels on the side of the fire-box, and to ascertain the height of water in the boiler. When opened, water or steam will escape, according as the level of the water is above or below them.

Gland. A bushing to secure the packing in a stuffing-box.

Grade. The inclination of a road; expressed either by the number of feet rise per mile, or by naming the distance passed in rising one foot; thus, a grade of 1 in 330, which is 16 feet per mile.

Gravity. The tendency which all bodies have to find the lowest level. The resistance in pounds, occasioned by the gravity of one ton on any grade, may be found by multiplying the grade, in feet per mile, by the decimal number .4242.

Grate. The parallel bars supporting the fuel in the fire-box.

Guides. Rods, or bars, lying in the direction of the axis of the cylinder, and guiding the cross head, to insure a perfectly parallel motion in the piston rod.

Hand Levers. Levers to work the main valves by hand.

Housing. See *Jaw.*

Induction Ports. Two passages on side of cylinder, to admit steam within it,—one port communicating with each end.

Jaw. A stand secured to the frame, to hold the box of an axle. The jaw must allow the box to slide up and down within it.

Journal. The part of a shaft or axle resting in the box.

Lagging. A wooden sheathing around a boiler or cylinder.

Lap. The distance which the valve overlaps on each end over the induction ports, when in the middle of its travel.

Lead. Distance to which the induction port is opened, when the piston commences its stroke.

Link Motion. An arrangement for working the valves, described in the body of the book.

Manometer. An instrument for determining accurately the pressure on a given surface, as a square inch, within the boiler.

Man Hole. A hole to admit a man within the boiler.

Mud Hole. A small opening at bottom of water space around fire-box, to clear out deposits of dirt, and other matter introduced with the water.

Packing. Any substance used to make a joint steam or water tight.

Pet Cock. A small cock between the check valve and pump, to see if the latter is working.

Pintal. An upright pin. There is a pintal secured beneath the forward end of the engine, to connect it with the truck frame, and to allow of the turning of the truck, independent of the engine.

Piston. See *Cylinder.*

Piston Rod. Rod secured at one end within the body of the piston, and at the other to the cross head. This rod passes through the cylinder cover, and is made steam tight by packing secured in a necking, or recess, outside of cover, and called a stuffing-box.

Plug, Fusible. A lead plug tapped in top sheet of furnace, to melt and give warning when the water falls below it.

Plunger. The solid piston of a pump, and pressing only by one end against the water.

Ports. Openings, or passages.

Priming. The passage of water, along with the steam, into the cylinders, when the engine is working.

Rocker Shaft. A shaft rocking in its bearings.

Reversing Lever. A lever in reach of the engineman, acting upon the valve motion, and to change the direction of the progress of the engine.

Safety Valve. A valve on the boiler, to discharge the surplus steam generated, above what is required for the engine, and which by accumulating would endanger the safety of the machine.

Slide. See *Guide.*

Smoke-box. A chamber at forward end of boiler, where the smoke and sparks from the tubes are received and discharged through the sparker.

Sparker, or Chimney. A pipe to discharge the smoke and waste steam, and surrounded by a casing to retain the sparks.

Springs. These are required over each wheel to reduce shocks and jolts.

Steam Chest. Box on top, or side of cylinder, and containing the valve to admit steam on the piston.

Steam Pipe. Pipe entering the dome, and communicating with the steam chests through two branch steam pipes in the smoke-box.

Stuffing-box. See *Piston Rod.* Used in all situations where a rod or spindle, having any end motion, requires to be made steam or water tight around same.

Sub-Treasury. A receptacle for sparks. Slightly different from those at the custom-house, but quite as beneficial.

Stroke. The distance travelled by the piston at each period of its motion.

Tender. A separate carriage, to carry wood and water.

Thimble. A tube of iron or steel.

Throttle Valve. A valve in the dome, and closing the mouth of the steam pipe.

Trailing Wheels. A pair of small wheels, placed behind the drivers, when but one pair of the latter is used.

Traction. Differing from adhesion in this: The adhesion is the power of the engine derived from the weight on its driving wheels, and their friction on the rails; while the traction is also the power of the engine, but derived from the pressure of the piston applied through the crank and radius of the wheel. These two elements may not always be the same.

Truck Frame. A separate frame, supporting four or six wheels, and turning on a pintal, independent of the body of the engine or car.

Tubes. These are used to conduct the heat from the fire-box, through the waist of the boiler, to the smoke-box. When a tube is so large as to require to be made of plates, riveted together, it is called a flue.

Valve. Any gate or fixture, other than a cock, to close a steam or water passage about an engine. The main, or port valve, which admits steam directly to the cylinders, is a block with a recess or cavity on its under side. The steam passes by the ends of the valve into the ports, and the motion of the valve, derived from the eccentrics, admits the steam at the proper time.

The uses of the cut-off and safety valves have been described.

The pump valves are either what are called, ball valves, spindle valves, or cup valves. The check valve is an additional valve on the forcing side of the pump, and is to prevent all danger of forcing back the water from the boiler into the pump, by the action of the steam.

Variable Cut-off. An arrangement to alter the travel of either the main, or cut-off valve, to use full steam through a greater or less distance of the stroke.

Variable Exhaust. An arrangement to enlarge or contract the blast pipes.

V-Hooks. So called from their form of opening;—much better than the common kind, as they are sure to catch the pins, and for this reason (though an old idea) are coming into general use.

Whistle. A hollow cup made to allow the steam to strike its lower edge, by which a shrill sound is obtained for signals.

INDEX.

www.ingramcontent.com/pod-product-compliance
Lightning Source LLC
LaVergne TN
LVHW021424110826
845150LV00007B/2071

* 9 7 8 1 4 2 5 5 0 8 1 6 6 *